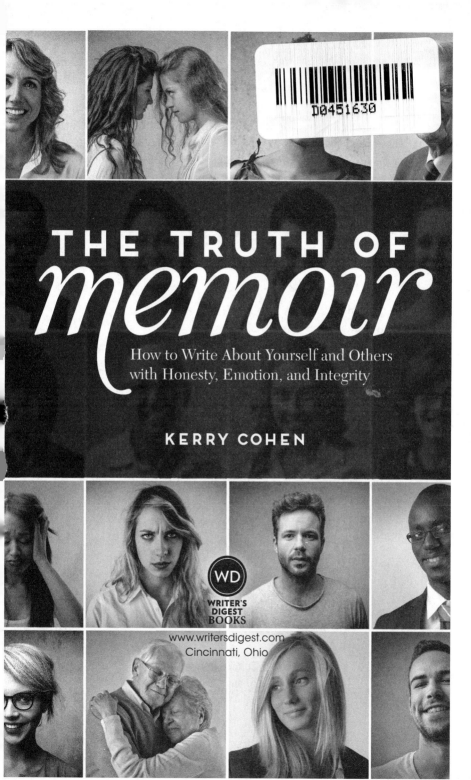

THE TRUTH OF
memoir

How to Write About Yourself and Others
with Honesty, Emotion, and Integrity

KERRY COHEN

WD
WRITER'S
DIGEST
BOOKS

www.writersdigest.com
Cincinnati, Ohio

For more resources for writers, visit www.writersdigest.com.

18 17 16 15 14   5 4 3 2 1

Distributed in Canada by Fraser Direct
100 Armstrong Avenue
Georgetown, Ontario, Canada L7G 5S4
Tel: (905) 877-4411

Distributed in the U.K. and Europe by F+W Media International
Brunel House, Newton Abbot, Devon, TQ12 4PU, England
Tel: (+44) 1626-323200, Fax: (+44) 1626-323319
E-mail: postmaster@davidandcharles.co.uk

Distributed in Australia by Capricorn Link
P.O. Box 704, Windsor, NSW 2756 Australia
Tel: (02) 4577-3555

ISBN-13: 978-1-59963-799-0

Edited by **Rachel Randall**
Designed **by Bethany Rainbolt**
Production coordinated by **Debbie Thomas**
Cover photos by **olly/Fotolia.com**

Dedication

For everyone who has a story aching to be told.

Acknowledgments

Thank you to all the wise, thoughtful memoirists who offered their words to serve this book. Thank you to Danielle Kutner, who helped me beyond measure in terms of making this book happen. I'd be dead in the water without her. Thank you to Rachel Randall, who believed in this book before it was one and who edited with wisdom and a sharpened pen. Thank you to James Bernard Frost for his support and love, to my parents who suffer through the fact that I continue to write about them, and to my children who give my life and life's work shape and meaning.

About the Author

Kerry Cohen is the author of the memoirs *Loose Girl: A Memoir of Promiscuity*; *Seeing Ezra: A Mother's Story of Autism, Unconditional Love, and the Meaning of Normal*; and *Girl Trouble*, which is forthcoming; as well as five other books. She teaches writing at the Red Earth Low-Residency MFA program, practices psychotherapy, and writes in Portland, Oregon, where she lives with her husband and their combined four children.

TABLE OF *Contents*

Introduction

A man I know wrote an essay about friendships after divorce that was published in a national online magazine. It doesn't matter whether the essay was well written or achieved its intentions or furthered thought on its subject. Those parts are at least somewhat subjective. Think, for instance, of Jonathan Franzen. Do you love his work? Do you not understand why others love his work? These types of reader perceptions don't matter for the purposes of this book. What *does* matter is that the essay the man published led to him losing his job. While he received many messages from people who found his essay helpful, moving, and relatable, a group of people in his local writing community were outraged because he wrote about three of them in order to further his point. Their names were changed, and no one outside of the local writing community would be able to infer their identities. But people complained and some made threats, and eventually the board of the nonprofit he worked for fired him, largely because of the essay.

A woman I know wrote an essay about her affair. She and her husband were still married, but she believed that the story of her affair and how she chose to end it was important for others, for the choices they might make. She believed that the realizations she had come to, having gone through the affair, were indispensable for others in similar situations. She published the essay obscurely, and she truly hoped her husband wouldn't find it. He wasn't much of a reader. He didn't find it. But someone who knew him did find it, and that person forwarded the essay to him in an e-mail. The writer and her husband are now divorced, and there are few things she regrets more in her life than having published that essay.

I have a story, too, albeit a very different one. I wrote my memoir *Loose Girl: A Memoir of Promiscuity* out of need. I could not *not* write it. Only after I sent it to my agent and he started shopping the book to editors did it occur to me what I'd done. I wasn't worried about the sex I discussed. I was worried about my parents. My God, my parents! I'd written as compassionately as I could about them, but they had both made terrible mistakes as parents. They were both very limited in their parenting, and as an adolescent, that affected me pretty seriously.

When the book was in review-copy form, I sent one to each of my divorced parents with notes of warning. I promised them that I had no intention of hurting them by writing the book. I explained that memoir is a story of one's own memories, and I did my best to stay true to my story, even if it hurt them and even if their memories were different from mine. My father was the first to get back to me. He joked, "Why would I read this book? It's a story of my daughter's sex life, and I come off like a jerk." He said it with a smile. It was his way of giving me his blessing. My mother took a different route. She read the book, and she surprised me by apologizing for that time in our lives. It was the beginning of a gradual openness in our conversations. It occurs to me now that had I not taken the risk of publishing *Loose Girl*, my mother and I never would have reached our current level of intimacy.

The power of words is astounding. They are just words: letters grouped together to make meanings that are knitted together to make a story. Memoir is really just a story about you and ultimately about others in your life. Words have the potential to injure or incense the people who are most important to you. But they can also transform lives positively.

Since I started giving talks and readings as a memoirist, and as I began teaching the craft of memoir, listeners and students continue to want most to know about this phenomena of writing about others. *How do I write about other people without hurting them, without losing people or things I love?* It would be easy to assume that one should write whatever they have to write, that they should publish whatever they want to put out there. But the truth is never so simple. Over the years, students have shared some of the terrifying potential consequences of publishing their stories. An ex-husband could take full custody of the children. A father could sue for millions. A daughter may estrange herself from her mother. The question is not about whether you, as a writer, have a right to tell your story. The question is whether art is more important than personal loss, whether the benefit to your readers, who are mostly complete strangers, is more important than someone you love, or even someone you don't love, getting emotionally hurt.

When students and readers ask me these questions, I often feel at a loss as to how to answer. The truth is that I don't know. Perhaps I lucked out when my parents supported me after *Loose Girl* came out. I still don't know how the book might affect my sons, whose friends might get wind that their mother wrote a book about sex. I also don't know how my second memoir about my autistic son will affect him or his brother as they grow. These sorts of questions tumble around in my mind, even as I move on to my third memoir.

I once told my students that they are hurting other people all the time anyway, so why not make art as they do? But I'm not sure that accepting the possibility that you will hurt people is the only solution to the problem of writing about other people. I believe that, like most problems, there are many approaches to handling the question of whether and how to write about other people, which led me to write this book. Herein, I interviewed close to sixty memoirists residing in the United States about how they dealt with the process of writing about those close to them. Their answers were enlightening, sometimes surprising, and always helpful. And the conversations were rich with tremendous passion for the craft of memoir.

We have no rule book for how to handle writing about other people, and certainly this book isn't one either. But in this book you will find the words and experiences of memoirists who have grappled with the myriad of questions and issues inherent to writing about others. Some may choose to read the book in its entirety, relishing and pulling wisdom from the many stories that memoirists shared for this book. Others may choose to read select chapters based on their own writing struggles. The book is broken down by specific subjects that memoirs may address: family, lovers and spouses, friends, children, sex and drugs. Included are thought-provoking essays by other writers about what happened to them as they wrote, completed, and published their memoirs and personal essays. I've also included a chapter that explores the legalities of including other people in your writing. At the end of each chapter, you'll find questions and exercises to help you explore your own memoir-writing process.

If stories can save, which I believe they can, then my greatest hope for my readers is that they find what they need in order to tell their own stories. Memoirs matter. Your story matters. But writing a memoir is also a tricky, tangled journey. My hope is that this book will help you head bravely into those woods.

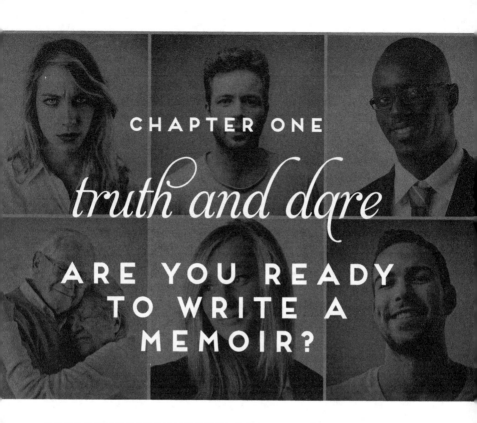

CHAPTER ONE

truth and dare

ARE YOU READY
TO WRITE A
MEMOIR?

"Memoir isn't the summary of a life; it's a window into a life, very much like a photograph in its selective composition. It may look like a casual and even random calling up of bygone events. It's not; it's a deliberate construction."
—WILLIAM ZINSSER, *ON WRITING WELL*

WHAT IS MEMOIR?

In the years that I've been writing and teaching memoir, I've found that many people don't quite understand what memoir is. It might be helpful to start by discussing what memoir is *not*. Memoir is not autobiography, which is a person's entire life story. I once had a student who thought that memoir was the same as autobiography. She started her book by detailing how she was born one evening during a snowstorm. Her plan was to write about her entire life, from birth until the present day. She had grown up in poverty in Mexico, immigrated to the United States, met a wealthy man who treated her badly, and had three children, all grown now. Eventually her husband had died, and she had moved back to Mexico, where she now hoped to write a book chronicling her journey. While talking with her, I suggested that no one in the publishing world would care about her whole life. She wasn't a celebrity of any sort, an Olympic medalist, or a well-known politician. She was simply a person, like you are, like I am, with a bunch of stories she wanted to tell. Unfortunately she assumed memoir was a good format to tell *all* of her stories, and she was deeply offended by my comments. But as Isaac Bashevis Singer wrote in *Love and Exile: A Memoir,* "Actually, the true story of a person's life can never be written. It is beyond the power of literature. The full tale of any life would be both utterly boring and utterly unbelievable." He refers here not just to the difference between autobiography and memoir but also to the fact that a memoir must be crafted and shaped, like clay into sculpture.

Here is another way to think about what memoir is not. Many times, people tell me, "I want to write a memoir because my life has been crazy/exciting/adventurous/horrible/unbelievable." But that's not a reason to write a memoir. It might be a reason to write fiction, but not a memoir. A memoir is not a collection of cool stories. It is not a chaotic or fascinating adventure. A memoir grows from the wild desire to make sense of what has happened to you. A memoir is, by definition, the story of the author's memories as he works to understand some aspect of his life.

Memoirs aren't just journaling, though. The words you write must matter beyond the page. By necessity of the genre, other people have to care about your story as they care about their own. As you make sense of your story, you're providing a way for others to make sense of their stories.

Many think the difference between memoir and fiction is that one is true and the other is made up, but memoir is actually more complicated than that. Journalists and historians aim to be factual. Memoirists do, too, but facts matter much less than the author's *experience* of the events. Mary Karr notes in *The Liars' Club: A Memoir*, "Memoir is not an act of history but an act of memory, which is innately corrupt." So even though a memoir tells the story of a person's memories, which conceivably are from real-life events that actually happened, not everyone will have experienced the events the same way. Your sister was there when Dad and Mom had that epic argument, but she might see it as one of the worst days in her childhood, while you saw it as the breaking point that finally led to their divorce, which freed you from their miserable relationship.

In Dani Shapiro's *Los Angeles Times* essay "Speak, Memory," she discusses her first efforts to write what eventually became her book *Slow Motion: A Memoir of a Life Rescued by Tragedy*. She unearthed her girlhood journals, thinking they would help her find the story, but she found that they weren't helpful at all—instead she found a bunch of sad, adolescent feelings that no one would care to hear. As Shapiro explains below, she found her story when she realized that her memoir's narrator wasn't that young Dani but the older Dani, the woman who made sense of the young Dani's life.

> I discovered that memoir is not a document of fact. It isn't a linear narrative of what happened so much as a document of the moment in which it is written. The present moment acts almost as a transparency, an overlay resting atop the writer's history. The interplay of these two planes—the present and the past, the me now and the me then—create the narrative and the voice. One can't exist without the other.[1]

---

1 www.latimes.com/entertainment/arts/la-caw-off-the-shelf26-2009jul26-story.html#page=1

The narrator—personified by that interplay between now and then—is what makes a memoir matter to its readers. The narrator is the one who allows the reader to care about the story and see herself on the page.

WHY WRITE A MEMOIR?

I noted above that we write memoirs to make sense of the things that have happened to us. We come back again and again to a theme, a concept, or a nagging notion about something we have experienced. In *The Liars' Club*, Mary Karr saw that her life had been shaped by storytelling. In *This Boy's Life: A Memoir*, Tobias Wolff came to understand that his stepfather's physical and emotional abuse led him to become who he is today. In *The Year of Magical Thinking*, Joan Didion recognized that the year following her husband's death was molded by her tendency to deny the loss. All memoirists use writing to understand their lives.

We also write memoirs to recognize the ways in which we are like others. When I was in graduate school for writing, my professor, the phenomenal writer Ehud Havazelet, said something that has since woven itself into my writing life: *Exile is the most human of experiences.* All human beings ache to be less alone, to be connected to others, and writers aim to do so through their work. Memoir writers are no different. We want to find that place in our art where our words allow intimacy with our readers. As they read our words, we want them to think, *Yes. That's it. That's exactly how I feel, too.*

We also write memoirs to enlighten others. We want to contribute to the dialogue about the human experience and find epiphanies, openings, and expansions in our understandings of others and ourselves. Lynn Beisner, who writes personal essays, explains how writing about yourself can shape your identity.

> The act of writing in and of itself has the power to reify ideas and the power to strongly shape what we remem-

ber or how we frame events. Micro-sociologists have discovered that the stories ... we tell ourselves about our lives, our internal biographies, literally shape our future. ... When you write a narrative about a relationship, you are deciding not just how you will remember it but also how it will impact your future. It is like pouring quick-drying concrete over a memory; it reifies something complex in just one of the many ways it could be viewed. And that is both the gift and the problem with writing our narratives.

We can also challenge accepted and repeated ideas about who we are. In other words, telling your story provides an opportunity to take on the cultural or familial narratives that have long been accepted as truth.

Memoir is often accused of being narcissistic, but this is a false assumption. The most important relationship in memoir is the one between the writer and the reader. The words on the page serve as a conduit for communication between these two parties. In other words, memoir focuses more on the people who will read the memoir than on the person writing the memoir.

With that in mind, memoir writers must determine whom they're writing for. Is the writing just for you? Is it to exact revenge on a certain family member? If so, you shouldn't be writing this memoir, at least not yet. Consider your readers. You want them to be engaged with the words, and you want them to put down the book having learned something about themselves or the world beyond.

ARE YOU READY?

Should you wait to write the memoir? There isn't an easy or "correct" answer to this question. Even if you've determined that you are writing your memoir for people besides yourself, you should reflect on several other factors before beginning.

EMOTIONAL STATE

First, consider your emotional state. Many memoirs are explorations of traumatic experiences. For example, Kathryn Harrison's book *The Kiss: A Memoir* describes the author's four-year incestuous affair with her father; *Jarhead: A Marine's Chronicle of the Gulf War and Other Battles* by Anthony Swofford recounts the hell of war in 1990s Saudi Arabia; *Down These Mean Streets* by Piri Thomas details the author's experiences with drugs, street fighting, armed robbery, and prison. These authors surely could not have written their stories while experiencing them; they all needed time to process what had happened to them.

For some, waiting to write leads to better crafting and understanding of the story. For others, waiting to write protects their emotional health; writing too soon would be traumatizing. Judy Huddleston, author of *Love Him Madly: An Intimate Memoir of Jim Morrison*, said, "Let the dust settle. You need more time than seems necessary to process major life events. It seems like I'm running two decades behind, which may be more than needed." Digging into messy memories will inevitably bring up discomfort, but writers should be aware of the real risk. If it drives you to a truly dark place, you should probably wait in order to develop more worthwhile reflections for both you and your readers.

Yet some others wrote their memoirs while living them. I did so while writing *Seeing Ezra: A Mother's Story of Autism, Unconditional Love, and the Meaning of Normal*, and as a result I captured the emotional freshness of my experience. Lynn Beisner recommends that writers be judicious when choosing the right time to begin a memoir.

> That is both the gift and the problem with writing our narratives. The stories ... we tell ourselves about our life are supposed to change over time. The perfect example of this is divorce narratives. In the year just after the end of a marriage, the story that a person is likely to tell him- or herself is likely to follow a very distinct pattern

and to be very emotionally charged. Ten years after a divorce, most divorce narratives are less black-and-white, less emotionally charged, and much more generous to both parties. When we commit to a narrative by writing about it and even further lock it down by publishing that account, we are in some ways committing ... to tell[ing] ourselves and others that story about our life for the rest of our lives. The gift about these locked-down narratives is that some stories need to be told and locked down before time fades them and leads us to remember either only good things or only bad things, depending on our disposition. Nostalgia does funny things to human memories, as we see in war stories. Ten years after soldiers fought in bloody, gruesome, and inhumane battles, they will somehow remember them as the best days of their lives. There are some narratives that need to be locked down before time scabs over the pain.

Every story needs to be told at a certain time, and each story deserves that consideration before it enters the world. The answer to when your story needs to be told is only partially based on whether you already have a completed arc in your life; you must also understand your emotional relationship with the material.

RESPONSES AND REACTIONS

When my agent finished reading the manuscript of my first memoir, he called me to ask, "Are you sure?" Was I sure? Of course I was sure! I had slaved over my computer for months. I had pulled out my hair for years before that trying to find the story I was desperate to tell. After the book came out, though, I understood what he had meant. I never could have guessed the responses I got from family, friends, and complete strangers, some phenomenally good, some truly horrible. You can't predict what reactions you will receive, but you can be guaranteed you will get some. Memoirists can (and often should!) change names and identifying details, but most people close to you, or previously close to you, will know whom you're writing about. Consider the following questions as you move forward with your project, all of which are explored in more detail in this book. The chapter or chapters listed in parentheses after the question indicate where you can find more information.

- Am I ready to take responsibility for my story (chapters one and two)?
- Do I need to consider waiting for certain people to pass away (chapter two)?
- Am I ready to reveal so much about myself, especially the bad stuff (chapters five and six)?
- Am I ready to expose other people's lives (chapters two, three, four, and six)?
- Am I willing to risk my job (chapters five, seven, and eight)?
- Am I willing to risk my reputation (chapters five and eight)?

However, maybe your project matters more than the potential reactions or consequences, and you want to get it out there. Maybe you have a way of looking at experiences that others would benefit from. Maybe your memoir could help your career, e.g., if you're a writing teacher or English professor.

Cheryl Strayed, author of the best-selling memoirs *Wild: From Lost to Found on the Pacific Crest Trail* and *Tiny Beautiful Things: Advice on Love and Life from Dear Sugar,* shared her experience of writing about her mother after she died.

> It's much easier to write about people after they're dead, the prime reason being, of course, that you can't hurt, offend, or enrage a dead person. You can tell your entire truth about him or her without directly impacting the relationship. There's a great liberation in that. In a strange way, their story belongs to you. Another layer is that if you do your work right—by which I mean your personal work,

your grief work, your emotional work, your forgiveness and sorrow and acceptance work—the death of a family member can allow you to understand things about the individual and your relationship with him or her more clearly and complexly than you likely would [have] if he or she were still alive. It sounds simple, but it's truly profound: When people die they are gone forever. It's the end. It isn't a breakup. It's never ever again, though your relationship with the deceased continues in another, interior and invisible, realm. Everything that happened in your life with that person is in the past, and yet your understanding of what happened continues to evolve and deepen over time. That gained wisdom will enrich your work as a writer. It can also be healing to write about someone who's no longer alive. My mom died when she was forty-five and I was twenty-two, and she's been a main subject in my writing over many years. I couldn't not write about her. I loved her so much I brought her back to life in my writing. I gave her back to myself by giving her to the world.

FICTION VS. NONFICTION

You own your story, but maybe memoir isn't the right form in which to tell it. A number of authors, including myself, have chosen to write versions of their stories as fiction. Kathryn Harrison did in *Thicker Than Water*. So did Dorothy Allison in *Bastard Out of Carolina*. So did many, many more. Fiction is as steeped in truth as any memoir. The difference is that you can make up your own ending. You can have your character live out your life slightly differently than you actually did. In the end, perhaps you care more about sharing the core truth of your story, which can be explored fictionally, than recording the precise events from which it is drawn. In fiction, you aren't expected to remember every detail of the conversation you had with your sister or whether you waited twenty or thirty minutes for the train. The core truth remains in the heart of the story, even if you alter events or details. However, keep in mind that in both fiction and memoir, the relationship you have with your audience is based on the understanding of whether this story actually happened.

Consider your story: Is it the general dynamic of the story that matters, or is your specific experience essential? What form is best for conveying the material? How will this story be told best? The only real difference between fiction and nonfiction is the audience and what they expect to understand about you and your experiences after closing the book. Your stated genre is a pact between you and your reader. This is your real story, or it isn't. Beth Kephart wrote, "When you draw from real life for the purposes of fiction, you have to be willing to discard details that have mattered deeply, to blur edges of the truth, to shape newly." Are you willing to do that with your story? If you choose to write a memoir, you are tacitly promising readers that you will be careful with their hearts, the subject matter, and the genre itself.

EXERCISES

1. Why do you want to write a memoir? Include your personal, interpersonal, and any larger societal motivations for your writing.
2. Write down your top concerns about your memoir. What are your fears? How might you and others benefit from your memoir?
3. Make a list of memories and events that you think are vital to your story. What makes each of these memories and events important to you and your narrative?
4. What aspects of your story do you think would resonate with others? Is there a larger social dialogue or universal experience that your memoir would be part of?

MEMOIR POSTPONED
Janet Clare

I was married to a writer. A good one, but who cares? I've never written a word about him, although of course, I have. From the safe distance of fiction, one of those things you just have to get out of the way. No longer bitter, too many years gone by for that. I never really hated him, even though he deserved it, deserved exposure. He'd had an affair, then confessed—after leaving evidence to be found—smiling hopelessly, goon faced, "She's young, and she loves me." Then he followed it up by paraphrasing Hemingway (because he was so very, very literary), "I wished I'd died before loving anyone else." Did he not know I'd read that line, too? Don't try to pass off stuff as your own. Here, now, midbattle. Unforgivable. I threw the requisite number of items across the living room. Mostly soft, nothing valuable, nothing I really cared about. Then I retreated silently. Went off, went on.

As a reader, I always adored writers. Fancied I might grow up to be one. But riddled with the usual insecurities and then married to what I'd thought of as the greater talent and a full-on narcissist, there was never enough room under the same roof, not enough air. And so I supported him. I created a business I knew nothing about. I worked hard. He didn't know how to find my office. He farted around. I trusted in his talent, not knowing history was littered with women who gave up or gave in to the so-called better artist. But sometimes you lost it all. Your own dreams and the ones you shared.

Several years after our divorce, he published a book. In a bunch of languages. Nonfiction. Historical. Hysterical. In a tailspin, upset at being upset, I saw a therapist. I was like the wife who put her husband through medical school and then he skips with nursie. After the end, it didn't end. I spotted him in Paris, thought

I was hallucinating. I traveled to Africa and he showed up, figuratively, but still spinning. I nearly fell off the elephant.

So, now what if I wrote the story, the real one? The one where he turned a blind eye while the famous English director he idolized put his hand under my skirt as the three of us boarded the fragile London elevator? Or the one where he careened down the street, drunk, and landed in a posh L.A. jail? Or, crème de la crème, how about the baby? Oh, yes, there was a baby. So many stories. Maybe it was time. What if I called him out? What would it matter? We no longer shared the same name. Not because I remarried, which I did. But because by now I had so many names, my choice as a writer was to string them all together like the Russians or go back to the one I was born with, to just me.

Delicious. This idea now rooting in my brain. Write a memoir. Dredge it up; bring it all back. To what end, I wonder. Not my style, self-indulgent. No one cared about the laundry list of my life. Boring. Or maybe not. Maybe funny, maybe harrowing, maybe okay.

Janet Clare escaped the garment business where she was owner and designer of a children's-wear company, a business for which she was neither trained nor schooled. Building on that premise, she went on to fulfill her lifelong desire to write, and five years later her first novel, *Afterthought*, was picked up by a New York agent. She thought her troubles were over. They were not. But too late; she was in it forever. Her short fiction and essays have appeared in print anthologies. A native New Yorker, she currently lives and works in Los Angeles, where she is completing her third novel and looking for a new agent.

BELIEVABLE
R. Bonwell Parker

I had sat on a killer story for a full five years after I first work-shopped it in a college writing class. I had been told the story on a road trip by a man who had a reputation for embellishing stories—my father—as we drove from Idaho to Ohio for his twenty-fifth class reunion. It was a great story, to be sure, with adventure, intrigue, romance, and just a few too many factoids that made him seem a far more influential person than the struggling shopkeeper who had raised me. Among the less believable parts of his story involved single-handedly founding the first thespian society in Columbus and blowing the town away when he cast as the lead in his first play a sociopathic thug whom the school locked in the basement during school hours. He claimed to have done this when he was sixteen.

I listened to his story for several hours, enjoying it as much as I would enjoy any fiction, as his story took him through more adventures than Forrest Gump, until he had to disappear after a standoff between him and an overzealous California sheriff. It was a well-told story, not only cohesive but memorable as well. Then, when we arrived in Columbus, he introduced me to his old high school friend, a convict who had been given a day release to attend the high school reunion. He refused to provide his real name and insisted that his prison time was just a cover for a se-cret CIA mission. My father and I sat with this strange man as he proceeded to corroborate the entire Ohio-based portion of my father's tall tale.

After the reunion, my father took me on a tour of the oldest standing theater in Columbus, and they even let him take me up into the rafters, where he showed me the grip directives written in white grease pen, in his handwriting, twenty-seven years earlier, when he had founded the theater as a teenager.

I told him that I had to write his story before it was gone forever. He was reluctant, as he wasn't sure if the statutes of limitations had expired on all of his offenses.

"Don't worry," I assured him. "Nobody is going to think your story is real."

As it happened, I was more right than I thought. I wrote his tale into a short story and presented it to the workshop at my school.

The criticism was consistent. "I'm sorry," each of them said in turn, "this story just isn't believable. I mean, I understand that it's a fictional story, but it just doesn't make sense." They struggled so greatly to accept the story that they didn't even comment on my style or structure. Their only advice was that I needed to take it down a notch before they could really accept the story.

The professor overseeing the workshop tried his best to provide some positive feedback. "You're obviously setting this in a sort of dystopian alternate reality," he told me. "But the feel of it is as if it took place in the sixties, or maybe the seventies, in our past. Perhaps you could add some futuristic technology or even put it on another planet, so we understand it's not supposed to be realistic?"

For three years, I struggled with the story. What fascinated me about it was the understanding that it was exactly what happened thirty years earlier. I didn't want to make it cartoonish; I wanted people to believe it. But how could I make it more believable when it was already based on a true story?

Eventually I shelved the story. I moved on to journalism, taking a part-time job as a music reviewer and setting aside my aspirations as a novelist. Five years later, I found out that one of my classmates from college was promoting his new book and would be doing a reading at Powell's Books. I went to the reading, unsure if he would remember me. Not only did he remember me, he picked me out of the crowd after he finished his reading.

"Robert," he greeted me, "how are your stories going?"

"I'm doing music journalism now," I told him, trying to sound excited about where my writing had gone.

"No!" he said. "What happened to your California story?"

"Couldn't make it believable," I said. "I'm surprised you remember it."

He gave me a look. "That was a crazy story," he said. "It's one of the few stories that has ever really stuck with me."

"Maybe I'll give it another shot," I said.

"Do!" he encouraged me. He gave me his card and told me to let him know when the story was done, and he offered to show it to his publisher.

Motivated by his words, I started spending my afternoons in the library, staring at a blank screen for hours at a time. He may have liked my story, but I was no closer to knowing how to write it. How do you make a story believable that nobody believes? After a couple weeks of futility, I went for the Hail Mary of book writing: I went to the "book-writing" section of the library to find help.

Find help I did, but not in the form of a book. Browsing through the section was a young, lean teenager in a striped shirt, scanning the rows of self-help books with a hunger in his eyes that I knew I hadn't experienced in years.

I'm not a social person, so I mumbled some incomprehensible sounds in an effort to excuse myself as I reached past him and pulled a couple of books off the shelf.

He looked at the books I'd pulled. "No, no, no, no, no," he said, taking one of the books out of my hand and putting it back. "She doesn't know what she's talking about. Her first piece of advice is 'meet with your editor daily.' Nobody that has lunch every day with an editor needs help with their writing; they're already there."

I mumbled something that was meant to be thanks and took the other book to my computer. He must have followed me, because as I sat at my computer, he was sitting across from me.

"My name's Tyrone," he said excitedly in a voice that I never could have used in a library, even if we were the only two people in the room.

"Robert," I said.

"What are you working on, Robert?" he asked.

I told him about the basics of my story, how I'd tried before but nobody found it believable.

"That's mad!" he exclaimed. "Okay, okay, let's start from the beginning. So he tells you this story on the road. Let's start there."

I had a voice in my head that had been firmly planted there by other writers I'd known, warning me not to tell him too many details of the story, lest he steal it for his own. But by that point, it was clear to me that I would never finish the story myself. If he did steal the story, it would mean he was a better writer than I was and deserved it, and it would have given me some closure to see it in print, even if my name wasn't on it. I told him the story in more detail from the beginning.

He listened to every word, his white eyes looming in contrast to his dark skin, staring at me for over an hour as I told him the story. As I finished it, he sat silently, looking at me.

"So," he said and sat in silence. "Okay. You've got to get some space aliens in there."

"What?" I said, though it wasn't the craziest suggestion I'd gotten for the story.

"Think about it," he said, "You got this guy with superhuman powers. He's smart, he's strong, and he's sexy, but why? Why is he the way he is?" He leaned in, his giant tan-irised orbs inches from my face. "Space."

I was at a loss for words. "So I just add space aliens as a vehicle for the whole story?"

"No, they stay there." He stood up and started pacing back and forth as I looked around to make sure none of the library attendants were coming to kick us out.

"Okay," he said, "so the aliens, they're watching the whole time. Because your hero, there's an interstellar war and he's their only hope."

"What?"

He continued, undeterred. "Because, you see: They made him. They made him in another time, and he's an android. So they put him back in the past—that's why it's all in the seventies. So you got this hip Austin Powers space assassin, but the aliens, they're on to him, so they send another android, like an evil android, but he doesn't know he's an android. They tell him androids are evil."

"This is a story about a guy who starts theater groups," I pointed out.

"He does that, but he does it while he's trying to take over. And that's why the cops are after him. And that's why there's the CIA guy there, because the government knows and they're taking sides."

"He's not actually CIA," I said. "He's just crazy."

Tyrone strode up to me, lifting me out of my chair by my shoulders. "Is he? Is he crazy? Or is he the only one who's right?"

Tyrone stared at me for a long time, unblinking, suspending me above my chair.

"Tyrone," I said as calmly as I could, "I think you're thinking of *Blade Runner.*"

"Yes," he hissed. "This story is our new *Blade Runner.* Come back tomorrow; we'll get started."

He released me. I stood next to my desk, watching as Tyrone left without another word.

I sat down at my computer and wrote an e-mail to my old classmate, the one who had actually been successful as an author. I thanked him for the words of encouragement, and I expressed regret that I just didn't think I could write the story. Either people thought it wasn't realistic enough, or it needed to be complete fiction. I closed up my computer and went home.

A month later, he wrote back.

"Robert," he wrote, "people can't deal with your story because they don't want it to be real. I'll be honest with you. I remember the story, and it's predictable enough. It's not like you are breaking any formulas. But I still remember that workshop, and all those others that kept talking about how your story wasn't believable … did it seem that they protest too much? The story is too real. They want you to add a body count of fifty or a spaceship so they can go to bed at night."

"Why would I write a story that nobody would want to read?" I asked him.

He replied promptly, "You write a story about the unwillingness to believe. Write a memoir about a writer who has to tell a story that nobody wants to hear."

The story evolved many times from that point, so I can't say I took anyone's advice exactly, but I started writing again, and that was what mattered. I stopped trying to find the line that my critics could accept. I tried to find the line they couldn't handle. I made my critics the antagonists of my story.

I wrote back to my old classmate a few times, but I never got any more responses. Ten years after I first heard the stories, I self-published it and sold tens of copies online, some of them even to people who weren't directly related to me. The first of them to post an online review of the book was succinct but complimentary: "The truest depiction of the era that I've read to date."

R. Bonwell Parker is the author of *The Bonfire Delegation*, a novel based in part on his father's stories, and his latest book, *Being Russian*, is a memoir of his experiences as an exchange student in post-Soviet Russia. He lives in Portland, Oregon, with his wife and daughter and can frequently be found writing in cafés and trains around the state.

CHAPTER TWO

blood on the page

WRITING ABOUT FAMILY

"You own everything that happened to you. Tell your stories. If people wanted you to write warmly about them, they should have behaved better."
—ANNE LAMOTT, *BIRD BY BIRD: SOME INSTRUCTIONS ON WRITING AND LIFE*

There is no more potentially contentious group than family. We all know that to be true. Holidays with family bring stress. Visits from parents prompt us to unlock the liquor cabinet. The person who grows up to be a writer or artist of another sort is almost always the family member who witnessed her family members at their worst—abuse, horrible fights, alcoholism, and so on. We were the ones who rarely spoke about what we saw, but what we saw ate away at our insides, begging to be told. We were the truth tellers, the light shiners, the ones who were eternally misunderstood. And here we are, finally, before our screens, our fingers both itchy and hesitant, ready to tell our truth.

As we discussed in the last chapter, some have suggested memoirs are "narcissistic" because a memoir is a book about the author. In reality, a memoir can never be just about the author; it has to also be about its readers. Marya Hornbacher, author of *Wasted: A Memoir of Anorexia and Bulimia*, says, "My story in isolation is just a story, but my story when it reflects the story of the people is a piece of communication." This sense of being in communication with your readers is true for all memoirs, and it is certainly true for memoirs about family history.

LAYERED PURPOSES

All memoirs must have layered purposes. Your memoir should be both about your complicated mother and the ways in which we raise girls in the twenty-first century. It must be about the obesity you fought as a child and the ways in which our culture contributes to people's struggles with weight.

Consider two classic family memoirs as examples: *The Liars' Club* by Mary Karr and *This Boy's Life* by Tobias Wolff. While Karr's book is about growing up with her wildly eccentric and, at times, disturbing parents, it is much more so about storytelling itself. The Liars' Club is a group of men, including Karr's father, who meet at the bar to exchange stories. The stories are rarely true, and through Karr's experience with the club, she learns that how you tell a story matters even more than the story itself. She learns that storytelling has the power to save her from her family's truths. In the end, Karr crafted a book with voice, narrative structure, and theme that is as much about how to tell a story as it is about the actual story.

Wolff's memoir is about the abusive, violent stepfather whom he battled as he grew into a man. He tells the story with a dark comedy and rawness that is both entertaining and upsetting. The story is also, though, about how this young man used his imagination to retreat from the abuse and how he wanted most to become the hero he believed himself to be in his imagination. Like Karr, Wolff saved himself through storytelling, but his salvation came less through the social act of storytelling than through the introverted fantasies he developed for himself.

Add to these considerations the question of your intention in writing about family. Is it to reveal someone for the liar she is? Is it to prove your side of the story? Kim Barnes's memoir *In the Wilderness: Coming of Age in Unknown Country* addressed her difficult relationship with her father.

> You must treat nonfiction characters with [the] same complexity and compassion as you do in fiction. Know what their greatest fears and desires are. *Know* your characters as the whole people they are. If you haven't reached that level of understanding with them, then you shouldn't be writing about them yet.

In other words, never write in order to get revenge or to hurt someone. Write only to understand. Perhaps Anne Lamott is right that if people didn't want to be written about, they should have behaved better, but that doesn't mean you should behave badly back. What you really want, I'm sure—what all writers want—is to grasp why people behaved the way they did, what their actions or words actually meant. Abby Mims, who has written a number of personal essays and has completed a memoir that has not yet found a home, describes writing about her mother's death from cancer, her sister's cancer, and her sister's psychotic break.

> I know the facts, but I'm still sorting out the story. None of this is material I wanted, but it's what I have, plus so

much has happened [that] I almost have to write the book to make sense of it.

HOW TO WRITE ABOUT FAMILY

How do you write about family? The answer to this question is the same answer for how to write about anyone, whether in fiction or non-fiction, whether writing about your parents or an acquaintance or an ex-spouse—*with compassion*. You must always write with compassion. But what does this mean exactly?

Writing about others with compassion means writing about them as whole people. Your parents are not just the ones who did those crappy things to you when you were ten years old. They are also people who were once children themselves, who also had parents who may or may not have done crappy things to them. They grew up in a Detroit ghetto and had to share a can of beans with three other siblings for dinner every night, or they grew up in a time when women were treated like possessions, or no one ever talked to them about sex when they were teens, or they were bullied as children, or they traveled extensively, or they had to learn to speak English in a strange, unforgiving country. The point is that your parents are also people. They are human beings whose life events informed who they became. And all human beings, including you and me, are flawed, limited, and endearing in their flaws, as well as wonderful and unique. No one is exactly like anyone else, and that is a great thing. It's surely at least part of the reason you're a writer.

This doesn't mean you have to address the entire context surrounding a person in your book or essay, but it does mean that you should take the time to know more about who that person is. There are a number of ways to do this. The most obvious is to interview that person or the people who know her. But even if you can't find out about a person's background, try to see the person's context as you explore your experience or memory of that person. Notice gestures that reveal vulnerability, insecurity, or other feelings behind one's actions. Does your mother keep checking herself in the mirror? Does she rearrange the silverware on the table? Does your friend say, "I'm so happy for you," but her smile is too big, disproportionate to the situation? Does your wife answer your questions about where she's been all night, but she keeps her back to you the whole time she speaks? Notice the humanness of the person. Actually, notice the humanness of *all* people. It will make you a better writer and a better person.

Keep in mind that you must write about *yourself* as a whole person as well. In *On Writing Well: The Classic Guide to Writing Nonfiction*, William Zinsser notes that to write memoir, you must write from forgiveness rather than victimhood. When you write about the things that happened to you, you have to do so as the protagonist, the one who acts, the one who chooses how the story gets told. As described earlier in this chapter, Tobias Wolff does this by focusing on the ways he lied. He fooled the people around him, but he writes about his actions with forgiveness for himself. Here he writes about the recommendation letters he forged from teachers to get into boarding school.

> It was truth known only to me, but I believed in it more than I believed in the facts arrayed against it. I believed that in some sense not factually verifiable I was a straight-A student. In the same way, I believed I was an Eagle Scout. ... And on the boy who lived in their letters, the splendid phantom who carried all my hopes, I saw, at last, my own face.[1]

The letters he wrote were lies, but they were also images of who he believed he could be, and he came to see them as himself. Because his childhood limited him in many ways, the reader finds his lies endearing. We want them for him, too. We, too, forgive him for what he does.

---

1 Tobias Wolff, *This Boy's Life: A Memoir* (New York: Grove Press, 2000).

Consider Cheryl Strayed's approach to writing a memoir.

> … if you're going to show anyone's ass, it better be your own. I'm ruthless with myself on the page and as gentle as I can be with others. I believe it's a writer's job to tell the deepest, truest truth. That's what I come to literature for, and the search for that deepest truth is the engine of my own writing, but I also feel a serious responsibility to those I write about. Their truth does not belong to me.

Abby Mims explains her writing philosophy similarly.

> The book I eventually wrote placed nearly all the blame on myself for the demise of our relationship, my depression in the wake of no longer being in the role of caretaker, and my general feelings of loss and being lost. [My mother] was engaged to someone new very quickly after her cancer, and I was entirely alone and felt left behind. She often did not behave well either in this process, but I chose not to write about it. I'm not sure exactly why, other than I believe when you are writing nonfiction, if you are going to expose the people around you, you have to be willing to expose yourself as much, if not more, or it feels like cheating to me.

Cris Mazza, author of a number of memoirs, also feels that the narrator's active involvement in the story is key.

> A story about a random victim of fate is not very interesting. Misfortune and triumph are archetypical memoir material but can be made deeper, more complex, and thought provoking if the narrator owns his or her participation and contribution.

Taking responsibility for your part in the story makes sense. But what if your memoir focuses on when you were a child or when you really were a victim of abuse or wrongdoing? Depicting yourself as a whole person on the page doesn't only mean recognizing your role in a bad situation. It means being emotionally authentic. It means showing all of yourself: the shameful parts, the embarrassing parts, the parts that you might regret or that you wish weren't true.

The horrible irony of writing about family is that you want to write with an honesty that you would *never* want your mother to see. You want to show your true self, which is rarely pretty. And yet, this presents another irony. Your true self, in all its imperfection, is a hundred times more beautiful than you think. In fact, when you write about yourself as equal to those who behaved badly, your reader thinks, *Oh, my gosh, I feel exactly the same way! This writer knows who I am!* And what your reader wants—what often drives readers to pick up memoirs in the first place—is to be seen.

TO SHARE OR NOT TO SHARE

When you write about family members, you tell a part of their story. Those who don't understand the memoir form (i.e., that it's the story of *your* memories, rather than anyone else's) might take issue with this. Of course they will! What actually happened is sometimes impossible to determine. Steve Almond, author of *Candyfreak: A Journey Through the Chocolate Underbelly of America* and *Rock and Roll Will Save Your Life,* says, "[Memoir] is a radically subjective account of events that objectively took place." In other words, your memory is often different from other people's memory of what happened. As Linda Joy Myers of the National Association of Memoir Writers explains, you must not let this common obstacle get in the way of your storytelling.

> People in a family are like slices of a pie, each with a different perspective. … Families often fight over what

"really" happened. Some fights are maintained for generations. To write, you need to put the family dialogue out
of your mind.

I was surprised when one of the men I wrote about in *Loose Girl* told
me that I'd gotten everything right, except that his kitchen was stain-
less steel, not white. When I had written about him and his Park Avenue apartment, I hadn't remembered details. I remembered the basics of what happened, the feel of his apartment. The color of the walls,
the color of his kitchen—these details mattered not even a bit to the
story. What mattered was that his family was wealthy, and his apartment stuck in my memory for that reason. That's what I tried to convey.

Victoria Loustalot, author of *This Is How You Say Goodbye: A Daughter's Memoir,* has a different opinion on rendering your memoir's facts.

> When you write creative nonfiction, you are allowed to
> make up everything but the facts. If you're writing a story
> about your kindergarten backpack and that backpack was
> blue, don't write that it was fuchsia.

Easy enough said, but for most writers, the color of the backpack isn't
what will upset others. However, if you claim that your sister stole your
pencil box out of that backpack, this is another matter entirely. *You* remember that she stole your pencil box, but she says it isn't true. Who
is right? In a way, you both are. In an essay on memoir writing called
"Memory Lessons," Rigoberto Gonzalez says, "Their stories might be
incongruent with mine, but they would be just as valid." All of these
stories are true, but only one is yours. You have a responsibility to be
as honest as you can.

Kevin Sampsell, author of *A Common Pornography: A Memoir,*
adds the following.

> I often tell new writers to embrace and acknowledge the
> fuzziness of memory without speculating on the facts.

> If you're unsure about something, it's still okay to write about it, but be clear that you're relying on memory.

Because of this issue, because family members aren't always going to love your memories of what they've said or done, many writers want to know if they should show their manuscripts to the people they wrote about. This may be wise, but as Sue William Silverman suggests below, it is probably best to wait until you've completed the work.

> During the writing process, try to ignore the outside world as much as possible. The most important thing is to get your story down on paper. Don't prejudge or worry what so-and-so might think. Then, after all the words are written, you can decide what your next step is.

Most writers would agree that it isn't a good idea to share what you're writing until you're finished. The writing process is sacred, almost magical. Introducing anyone else's voice into your process is rarely a good choice for the work, an idea with which Kim Barnes would likely concur.

> I would talk to [family members] about what I was writing but in a general way, not with detail. It's not what happened [that matters] as much as *why*. It's not the details of the event but why you remember it the way you do.

Once the story is written, though, some memoir writers do choose to let their family members read it. Before she publishes a work, Hope Edelman asks certain family members who appear in her book for feedback about passages relating to them and sometimes offers them veto power. "This often improves a piece and sometimes leads to conversations we need to have on a personal level," she adds. Jay Ponteri, author of *Wedlocked: A Memoir,* shared with his mother and father the parts of his book that were about their failed marriage.

I showed my mom the essay I'd written about her marriage, and even though she was proud of me and liked the prose, she wasn't comfortable about how the work portrayed her. I made some slight changes to the work. Mostly, I [made changes by] acknowledging that my perceptions of her, my dream of her was [in reality] a dream of my own loneliness. Soon after, I told my dad about the book. He didn't even know the book existed. This was a blow to him. He was trying to be supportive of my work, but he was seriously confused as to why I'd publish a book that so openly talked about something that was, for him, a very private (thus silent) matter. I reread the sections about my parents' marriage and removed some things I thought might upset him. The sentences I cut out described my youthful, college-aged anger at him. I felt they could be taken out without compromising the work as a whole. I also fully cut out any mention of my dad's second wife.

But Abby Mims has very different advice. She said to me, "Never show anyone something you've written about them, before or after publication." In other words, don't go out of your way to let them know you wrote about them. They'll find out, or they won't. Robert C. Rummel-Hudson seems to agree.

Honestly, I regretted making changes in order to soothe relations with my in-laws. They never entirely let go of their resentment for my original draft, and the changes I made weakened the book measurably.

Ultimately you must decide whether to show the story and to whom you show it on a case-by-case basis. I gave my sister *Loose Girl* to read before it went to copyediting, because I'd written about her throughout the book and I wanted to respect her experience of becoming one of my subjects. Also, my sister is an artist and avid reader, and I trusted that she understood my intentions—that it was the story of *my* experience growing up in our family, not hers. Indeed, that's exactly how she responded. She was sad to read about my struggle, even if she viewed herself very differently. But she understood that if she wanted to show her reality, her perspective, she'd have to write her own memoir. And as a comic artist, she's done just that. I didn't trust that my parents would be quite as understanding, so I didn't tell them about the book until it was in advanced-reading-copy form and too late to make radical changes.

The bottom line is that no one knows better than you who to trust and who not to trust when it comes to family. Proceed with caution, and always, always, amid kindness to others, protect your work's integrity.

GHOSTS AND SKELETONS

Some of my students have told me that they simply won't write about their parents until they are dead. This can make sense, of course, especially if your memoir includes portrayals of your parents that are less than flattering—they abused you or neglected you in some way or suffered with mental illness or addiction.

But even if your parents are deceased, writing about them isn't necessarily easier. When Sue William Silverman wrote about her parents, they had already passed, but that didn't free her of obligation or guilt.

> Even though my parents were dead, there were concerns about protecting their reputations, say, among our relatives—and even my father's former business associates. (He had a rather high-powered career.) I felt a little guilty.

Judith Barrington also struggled with writing about certain family members after they died.

> At first I thought I was lucky since my parents were not living and would never read the book, but as I went on, I realized that writing about dead people is difficult in very similar ways to writing about the living. I felt a responsibility to how I presented them, and, even though I wrote honestly of my anger at my father, I tried not to lure the reader into taking my side.

While it may initially feel easier to wait until people are deceased, the process of writing and publishing truths about people will always be challenging. Both Silverman and Barrington note that what they write about their deceased parents will dictate, to some extent, how they will be remembered, and Barrington confesses that this makes it even *harder* to write about them than if they were still alive. It seems less fair to allow family members no recourse to defend themselves, should they feel the need. Also, you really don't know what a person's reaction to your story will be. You might be surprised. And it would be a shame to refrain from writing your story if in the end you had nothing to worry about in the first place.

WHAT TO EXPECT WHEN WRITING ABOUT FAMILY

People who set out to write a memoir about their families are often terrified of the possible repercussions. *What will Mom do when I out her as an alcoholic? What will my brother think of me once I tell what really happened between us? How will Grandma react to my feelings about her?* These are real, frightening questions, and many people become paralyzed at their keyboards, unable to write a word.

Sue William Silverman offers the advice below.

> I never allowed concerns to stand in the way of writing. I've always felt that as a writer of memoir, I own my truth and I am free to write about it. I don't feel that my job as

> a writer is to protect people. I don't feel my job as a writer
> of memoir is to make people feel comfortable. My job is
> not to sugarcoat life experience. I firmly believe in my
> right to tell my own narrative, which is exactly what I did.

We can't know how family members will react to the exposure of painful secrets or unspoken truths, but most memoirists would agree that you can't predict who will feel good or bad about the revelations in your work, and why. I thought one of my memoirs served as a sort of apology to someone, and that person is one of the people who couldn't forgive me for writing it. I was terrified about how my mother would respond, and she's been one of my greatest supporters. We can't know, nor control, what happens. The key, then, is to write. Just write, and prepare for potential responses, either good *or* bad.

NEGATIVE RESPONSES

Sometimes family members will be upset by the words you write. This happened to Jillian Lauren after her memoir *Some Girls: My Life in a Harem* was published.

> The biggest sadness was my parents' reaction to the memoir. I had hoped they would be able to be supportive, but I was also prepared for them to have a negative reaction. When the book came out, they were hurt and angry, and they opted to no longer have any contact with me.

Some of Victoria Loustalot's family also responded negatively after Loustalot's memoir about her father, who kept his sexuality secret and eventually died of AIDS, arrived on bookshelves.

> The only relationship that has really changed is the one I have with my grandparents. But I reached out to them, and we're talking now, and I think things will continue to

get better. I hope they will. I love them very much, and I don't want to lose them.

Abby Mims spoke to me about the price she has paid for her writing success.

> Would I rather have a relationship with my sister than this material, not to mention a healthy, live mother [referring to her mother's recent passing from cancer]? Of course. But right now, I don't see any way of repairing what has happened between my sister and me.

POSITIVE RESPONSES

Family members' reactions aren't always negative. In fact, I would argue that positive changes in relationships are just as likely. Consider Kevin Sampsell's account of his family's reaction.

> I think the memoir broke down a few walls within my immediate family. One of my nieces wrote to me and explained that her dad (one of the brothers I wrote about) wasn't as much of a family man [as] I thought. I spoke with her quite a bit about it and about her life, and it was really nice.

Loustalot was also pleasantly surprised by some of her family members' responses.

> My mom was apprehensive about this project before it was published. Even after she'd read it and agreed with my account, she was still nervous. Totally understandable. However, after the book came out, she started getting excited responses from her friends and family, and then she loved it. She's really enjoying her mini-celebrity status in our hometown.

Kim Barnes, whose father had shunned her before she wrote *In the Wilderness,* was sure that he'd do so again and that her kids would lose their grandparents. Her parents' response was a tremendous surprise.

> Mom cried because she was guilty that she hadn't done a better job protecting me from Dad. I said, "Look at me, I'm happy. I have a great life." We had a long convo, and then she cried for her own lost self. We always worry how others are going to react. Sometimes, though, if you're trying to understand people's stories, even showing their flaws, there's a kind of gratitude there. It's the first time anyone had ever tried to understand my mother's story, so instead of being angry, she was grateful. Someone had taken her seriously as a person with needs and desires, who was doing the best she knew how to do with what she had.
>
> Mom said Dad would call me next, which was surprising because he never used the phone. I curled up in bed waiting for what was going to come. When he called, he said, "You are my daughter, and you made a terrible mistake." There was a long pause in which I believe now he made a different decision. His voice changed, and he said, "You should have called me, because I could have told you what year your uncle's Chevrolet was." We talked for four hours.
>
> What I know now is that by allowing yourself to be vulnerable and flawed and compassionate, other people feel the desire to do the same thing. Those phone calls were gifts. They changed my entire life for the better. We cannot underestimate the love and permission that our families will give us if we believe in what we're doing for the right reasons.

The point Barnes makes is so important. You can't begin to know what will come from your writing, and you usually can't predict others' experiences. One memoirist I know says, "Whatever you think will happen, I can almost guarantee you it will be something else." Like Anne Lamott famously said, "If you really want to make God laugh, tell her your plans." And, sometimes, nothing happens. Susan Senator is just one of a number of people who told me there were no repercussions for their memoirs. She said, "No one was surprised—at least no one told me they were." This was my experience as well. My family members already knew me. They weren't shocked that I would write books telling my experiences. When had I ever *not* shared honestly about my experiences? When had I ever shied away from difficult truths? I could almost hear the sighs from my family members: *Well, of course. Here it is. We can't say we didn't know it was coming eventually.*

However, Alison Bechdel tells a story in her essay "What the Little Old Ladies Feel: How I Told My Mother About My Memoir" about how, after her memoir *Fun Home: A Family Tragicomic* was released, her mother sent her a review from a local paper. In the review, the writer referenced a William Faulkner quote: "The writer's only responsibility is to his art ... If a writer has to rob his mother, he will not hesitate." Bechdel explains that her mother's implicit endorsement of this review left her feeling conflicted about herself and her work.

> I do feel that I robbed my mother in writing this book. I thought I had her tacit permission to tell the story, but in fact I never asked for it, and she never gave it to me. Now I know that no matter how responsible you try to be in writing about another person, there's something inherently hostile in the act. You're violating their subjectivity. I thought I could write about my family without hurting anyone, but I was wrong. I probably will do it again. And that's just an uncomfortable fact about myself that I have to live with.[2]

---

2 Alison Bechdel, "What the Little Old Ladies Feel: How I Told My Mother About My Memoir," *Slate*, March 27, 2007, accessed July 21, 2014, www.slate.com/articles/news_and_politics/memoir_week/2007/03/what_the_little_old_ladies_feel.html

Compassion. Honesty. Forgiveness. Hold these words in your mind as you write about your family. Allow them to pulse through the pages of your memoir. Know that you can't presuppose how your family members will react to your writing about them, but if you keep these precepts in mind, you will reduce your chances of hurting or angering them. But let's face it—you'll never find out how they'll react if you don't write it.

EXERCISES

1. Choose one family member featured prominently in your memoir. Write two short scenes consisting of your best and worst memory of this family member. How do your portrayals of him or her in the two scenes differ? How might these two exercises inform your portrayal of the family member in your memoir?

2. Write a scene in your memoir from the perspective of the person in your family you are most afraid of writing about. What happens to the scene when it is skewed toward someone else's reality?

3. Imagine you're going to discuss a scene in your memoir with a family member featured in it. What might they take away from the scene? What are the key things you're trying to communicate in the scene? In what ways might your intended and received message be similar and different?

4. Read one of the scenes you found particularly difficult to write. Are there any instances where you notice yourself writing cautiously? Do your inhibitions come from a place of fear? Are you leaving out important details or aspects of the scene? How might the narrative change if you include these details or aspects?

5. Write a scene consisting of an interaction you witnessed between other family members such as a family dinner or a holiday gathering. Do you catch yourself telling the reader that "my sister felt ..." or "my father acted ...?" How could you illustrate these things through your family members' behavior or dialogue, rather than telling the reader?

6. Pick a memoir that focuses on a family secret. What makes the secret a "family secret"? How does keeping the secret affect each of the characters in the book?

7. Pick a memoir that focuses on a family secret. Imagine you're reading the memoir from the point of view of someone keeping the secret. How does it feel to have that secret exposed?

WRITING MY SISTER REAL
Ona Gritz

I couldn't write about Angie—her life or her death—until everyone else in our immediate family had died. Not that I planned it, waiting ghoulishly, ticking names off a list. I simply never imagined trying to capture my sister's story on paper. It was too painful. Too complicated. It would upset too many people. Besides, I'd locked the details of her life away so thoroughly, and so long ago, that I probably couldn't access them if I tried.

Then one rainy morning, two-and-a-half years ago now, I heard what had once been a favorite song of hers on an oldies station. *I'm the only person alive who knows she loved that song*, I thought. And what occurred to me next, as though she'd bent and whispered it in my ear, was that she deserved to live in a bigger place than my faulty memory. *You're not a writer for nothing, Baby*, I nearly heard her say.

The thing is, that song—*My Baby Loves Love*—had been a hit. I'd heard it countless times over the years, and while it always reminded me of my sister, it never before came with a call to write.

But something big had happened since the last time I'd stumbled upon that snippet of nostalgia on the radio. My half-brother, Steve, lost a years-long battle with cancer. He and I had been the sole survivors of our nutty, disjointed clan. His father had died of a stroke a decade before. Not long after, our sister Tina (his whole, my half) had succumbed to hepatitis C. Then my parents (our mom, my dad) died of cancer within two months of each other. And, of course, Angie—the one sibling I grew up with, the one I imitated and fought with and followed around the house— had been the first to go, murdered at twenty-five, along with her husband, infant son, and the nearly full-term baby in her womb.

I'm the only person alive who knows she loved that song. A heartbreaking realization—*I'm all she has*—but also a freeing one. If I were to explore Angie's story and commit it to the page, there was literally no one left who might be wounded, made raw or furious by what I revealed.

***

I had been with Angie and her family the day before they died. I'd met the "friends" who were later convicted of killing them. Yet I knew very little about what had happened. *Just the facts, ma'am,* a television detective said on a show Angie and I watched in re-runs as children. The facts—skeletal, unadorned—were all I could handle. A few words I could recite quickly, without really hearing them, before changing the subject. *My sister and her family were murdered by a couple who were staying with them. Yes, I know. It was awful. Do you have any brothers or sisters?*

But now that Steve was gone, a brother I grew to know and love in adulthood, I felt a renewed longing for my sister. There was no bringing her back, but writing would be a way to spend time with her.

Even after thirty years, the facts surrounding a quadruple murder can be found, some right on the Internet. Others I uncovered from news articles I read hunched before a microfilm reader. Still more I learned from trial transcripts. And I talked to people. I called the man who had been my sister's landlord and who, one late February afternoon, cleaned out the long-neglected crawl space beneath the building and found my brother-in-law's decaying body. I interviewed the attorney who spent day after day in a courtroom, working to ensure that the killers were locked away for good. I sought out my brother-in-law's two brothers and introduced myself. *We're the same*, I kept thinking during our long hours on the phone. *My loss was their loss, too.*

Here are some things I learned from the articles and transcripts. Angie's body was found in a nightie, panties, and a single slipper. My brother-in-law had been hog-tied before he was shot. By the time my nephew's remains were uncovered, he no longer had a face. The unborn baby, removed from my sister's womb by a coroner, would have been a girl.

And here is something I learned from talking to people. I was wrong in thinking it was safe now, wrong in thinking everyone affected by my sister's story was gone.

When I was six and Angie—whom we still called Andra—was twelve, she ran away from home. There was a song she'd taught me that looped through my mind during those long nights I slept alone in our shared room. *The cat came back the very next day. They thought he was a goner, but the cat came back* ... It was my version of a prayer, and it worked. My sister did come back, in dirty, unfamiliar clothes and with a new knowledge of the world I could sense by looking in her eyes. After that, running away became something she did—frequently. She was here, gone, here again, until I came to feel she only existed in my presence; her life simply halted in the in-between times as if someone hit the pause button on a tape player.

At twelve, Andra was precocious, womanly, a notorious bad girl. The way my parents explained it, running away was yet another thing bad girls did. They stole change from their mothers' pocketbooks. Snuck cigarettes. Did "God-knows-what" in the hidden corners of school yards with boys. They ran away.

I believed all of this. Despite that no one else I knew had a runaway for a sister. Despite that our mother, who coddled and adored me, only ever scolded Andra, scowled at her, and, once, chased her through the house and beat her with a metal dustpan while I screamed at her to stop.

Context. Motivation. Backstory. These are things I think about as a writer. If a child runs away from the safety of home, it's likely that home is not actually safe. I know this, and yet I never applied this knowledge to Andra. Before I started to write her story (at forty-nine!), I thought of her with the mind of a baby sister. Andra was here, gone, here, finally gone for good. The cat came back, and then it didn't. Andra began leaving for the wide-open dangerous world at twelve because she was wild, a runaway. It's why she got killed, because it was in her nature to fly toward danger. My parents had told me that, too, when I was nineteen and my sister's body in its nightie and one slipper were discovered. Believing them was the quickest way to close the door on the horror of what had happened and on the shameful fact that I failed to save her.

Now, finally, the door was propped open—by a song and a longing for the girl who had been my first love. A girl who clearly had run away because she needed to. She needed to remove herself from her mother's, *our* mother's, *my* loving mother's, abuse.

But where did my mother's venom come from? Going by my experience alone, it had always been there. *Stop it, Andra*, I grew up hearing my mother hiss. I watched her frown whenever my sister spoke to her, even if Andra was simply relaying a funny story from school. Worst of all, I learned early that I could set my sister up. *She bit me!* Andra complained to our mom one rainy afternoon. I had. I'd bitten her hand. But our mom responded the way I knew she would. *Oh Andra. Leave her alone. She's just a little girl.*

***

Writing about Andra meant facing that awful ending, but it also meant uncovering the beginning. The part of her story that predates my earliest memory of the two of us side by side on a bench on a boardwalk, the salty breeze tossing our hair into our eyes. I was probably three then, which would make her nine. When she was six months old, my parents—a hitherto confirmed bachelor and a divorcee with two children living on the opposite coast—adopted her and brought her home. I needed to understand Andra's life in that window when she was our parents' only shared daughter.

Miraculously, Andra's junior high still had her records. I pored through them, watched *B*s turn to *C*s, a *helpful child* become someone who gets into fights. Midway through, I found myself on the page, in a note by a counselor who saw Andra in sixth grade. *Seems unhappy at home. Feels mother loves "real" sister, not her.*

I swallowed hard, left the papers spread on the floor, took the dog for a long walk. I'd been the favored one, my parents' surprise midlife baby, their child by blood. And just as I feared, I'd been the root of Andra's despair.

Due to a series of feuds and splits, Andra and I grew up barely aware of our extended family. We had cousins, but we rarely saw them. Now I sought them out. Strangers to me who knew my sister before I did. Three cousins, surprised yet seemingly pleased to hear from me. Deeply affected by the murders. Willing to talk.

Rachel had never seen a mother show less interest in a little baby. "I was just a kid when they brought her over, but it left such an impression on me I wrote a paper about it for a psychology class in college." Lois remembered my mom letting Andra roam the neighborhood unattended when she was no more than a toddler. Lauren recalled her leaving Andra outside to play alone on the stoop in bitter cold December while she cleaned the house.

My mother as villain. My mother as victim. She had divorced her philandering first husband in the unforgiving 1950s. "No one got divorced in my day but Elizabeth Taylor," my dad once said. He didn't want the neighbors to know his wife had been previously married. Nor did he want to be a stepfather. He craved a fresh start, so my mother's children were sent to their father. But that fresh start didn't go as planned. Two miscarriages. A baby who died in days. Finally, the adoption. My mother's assent was clearly begrudging. She had children, and she'd given them up. If she tried at all to love her new daughter, she failed.

In photographs my sister is a beautiful baby. Bright, curious eyes, white-blond hair, puckish smile. After hearing what my cousins witnessed, I wanted to pluck her out of each picture, pull her through the decades, and take care of her. At the same time, I felt the release of something ancient and heavy. The issues predated me. My birth wasn't the thing that ruined my sister's life.

Still I remained haunted by that note in her school records, *Feels mother loves "real" sister, not her.* Regardless of what came before, I was named and implicated in her misery. And there was something else about that quote that tugged at my insides. Its odd phrasing. In those days the language of adoption emphasized separateness, artifice. One's birth mother was one's *real* mother. Andra, in talking about us, took this even further. The counselor—I can tell by her placement of quotation marks—noticed this, too. In Andra's mind, I was real. She was not.

Years later, in reaction to the murders, I made that true for myself as well. I closed myself off from our shared history, made her as thin as a paper doll. Only by putting words on the page have I begun to change that. As I write I feel her long fingers poking lightly at my ribs. See her smile twist as she holds back a laugh. Hear the earnestness in her voice as she explains her side of an argument. Note the pride with which she announces, "This is my baby sister."

As of this writing, I'm in the midst of editing the manuscript. It's very much a work in progress, and there's no knowing what may come of it. Except that it's already given me this gift—made my sister real to me again. My goal, now, is to make her just as real to you.

Ona Gritz is a columnist for *Literary Mama* and co-poetry editor of *Referential Magazine*. Her essays have appeared in *More*; *The Utne Reader*; *New York Family Magazine*; *Brain, Child*; *Bellingham Review*; and elsewhere. She is the author of two poetry books, two children's books, and, most recently, a novella-length memoir, *On the Whole: A Story of Mothering and Disability*. Ona is currently at work on a memoir, tentatively titled *Everywhere I Look*, about her sister's tumultuous life and violent death.

TALKING SH✳T ABOUT THE DEAD
Ariel Gore

I have this recurring nightmare that my mother is alive.

She never died.

I've made a terrible mistake.

I have to call my editor.

We can't publish the book.

I don't know how I could have made such a wild mistake.

I mean, she *looked* dead.

I signed the papers.

I let the man from the cut-rate crematorium in Albuquerque take her body away.

But in the dream she isn't dead.

And in the dream, she's *really* pissed about the book.

I can't get through to my editor. Of course I can't get through. It's too late. It's already out, anyway. My editor can't do anything.

Maybe I can hide the books.

Or.

Maybe.

Just walk away.

I'd been having the dream for nearly six months the night it occurred to me: It didn't matter if she was alive.

If I'd lived these many months believing she was dead, feeling freer because she was dead, writing the truth without worrying about cleaning it up because she was dead, then who the fuck cared if she was alive—or pissed?

***

I wrote my first memoir, *Atlas of the Human Heart*, when my mother was still very much alive. Oh, it seems like eons ago. Even my stepdad was alive. Was it only a decade? It was my favorite book to date. The story of running away from a suburban adolescence full of rich bitches, tortured punks, drugs, and sexual violence to travel around Asia and Europe, in and out of love and danger. It was the story of learning, as Muriel Rukeyser says, that the only security that matters is the security of the imagination. It was the story of becoming a teen mom.

It was not a story about my parents, but they appeared briefly in the narrative. And because I was my mother's daughter, and because I'd been trained, all my life, to stay silent about her particular brand of meanness and abuse, I went to great effort to clean her character up.

And so it was that she hardly appeared in the book, and, where she did, she seemed to behave better than she actually had.

Still she read each page as a betrayal.

I'd been so excited to show her that book.

I'd imagined, somehow, that she would be proud of me. Imagined, even, that she would call it poetry. Imagined that she'd think I was brave.

"You made me throw up," is what she said when she slammed her copy down on my dining room table. "How could you do this to me?"

I didn't say anything.

"How could you do this to your daughter?" she demanded. "How is this supposed to make *her* feel?"

That's when I knew I had written no poetry.

I had written something shameful.

I thought about the review copies that were already out, the tour dates I'd already planned. But now I hoped that not so many people would read my book.

"I've called John," she announced, then shook her head. John. My stepdad. I loved him like a Sierra mountain trail. "I've forbidden him from reading this. It would kill him, Ariel."

Maybe it's ironic that, a few years later, my mother was the one to kill my stepdad.

And it took poison, not a memoir.

"You shouldn't have bothered cleaning her up," my sister said. "*Atlas of the Human Heart* would have been a better a book if you'd admitted to all the reasons you ran away. And she couldn't have been any more pissed off."

And maybe my sister was right.

My mother was already dead when I started writing *The End of Eve: A Memoir*, but she'd only been dead a couple of weeks. From a mental-health perspective, I probably should have waited longer. Maybe time would have staved off the nightmares. But from an artistic perspective, I knew I couldn't wait. Very soon after my mom died, I found myself beginning to sugarcoat the whole experience. I told myself, *Well, maybe it wasn't all that bad.* That's when I knew I had to get the story on paper as soon as I could. Part of the reason there are so few stories about the hard and crazy part of caregiving for the dying is that our culture teaches us to "get over it"—which is a kind of forgetting. I didn't want to forget.

The culture also teaches us not to talk shit about the dead.

It's quite the nullifying paradox of abuse culture, if you think about it. We're not allowed to speak truth about our experience with violence or power plays when the players are alive. I mean, we wouldn't want the neighbors to find out.

But we're certainly not allowed to speak of it once they're dead.

Death renders everyone a saint, doesn't it?

And they're not even here to defend themselves!

Here now in America—and probably in the world—so many times "family" means a code of loyal silence.

I'm not here to tell anyone whether they're ready to break their own personal and familial and lover codes. Not every private vulnerability cries out to be made public.

When my mother was dying, really dying finally, and bedridden and on plenty of morphine, she asked me, "Do you think memoir-writing is a way to express anger or a way to pay tribute?"

At the time I told her, "Probably both." But in reality I think it's something bigger than that. Ideally the people you write about in a memoir won't read it. That's not who it's for. Memoir isn't about processing our relationships with one another. It's about integrating the enormity of everything. It's about taking the traumatic, disparate moments of life that are scattered around us and sewing them back together into something beautiful that maybe emboldens people who are going through the same thing—which we all are—because the "same thing" is life and it's hard and fucked up and delicious.

The only goal I had when I agreed to take care of my mom was to behave in a way that I would be proud of. And some days I did and some days I didn't, and I wanted to write *The End of Eve* not as a tribute or an exposé but as something else, as, *Hey, this is who I am and this is what I tried to do, and you might try to do the same thing one day and I have an idea that if I tell you—some stranger who lives on the planet with me—the story, it might free us both from our self-consciousness and our isolation.*

Last night I dreamed my mother was alive.

My stepdad was there, too.

But there wasn't anything about my book in the dream.

I wasn't frantically trying to call my editor, trying to call something off.

For once.

My mother was just looking for a blank canvas.

My stepdad was making vegetable soup.

We were what we were so often in life—the scenes that never make it into books—just living the everyday moments between the violent breakdowns and dramatic escapes. Just looking for a canvas. Just making soup.

Ariel Gore is the editor of *Hip Mama* magazine and the author of nine books of fiction and nonfiction, including the memoirs *Atlas of the Human Heart* and *The End of Eve*. She teaches writing online at literarykitchen.com.

WHOSE TRUTH IS IT ANYWAY?
Traci Foust

Someone once said, "Never let the truth get in the way of a good story." But what if the truth would make an even better story and you've decided to leave it out anyway? Because you're not just a memoirist; you're a nice person, you love your family, and you know they will understand and appreciate how meticulously you wrestled with all those things you have chosen *not* to say. The people you love will love you even more for everything you left out. After all, it took just as much effort and discipline to delete that harrowing scene about the time you walked in on your father and his mistress as it did to write about that family trip to Disneyland where nobody fought in the car. Sure, Dad getting it on with the babysitter is much more intriguing than playing slug bug with your little brother in the backseat of a Buick, but it's okay. You've done the right thing. Certainly the people in your life will thank you for this. Maybe. Just don't count on it.

One of the most common difficulties a memoirist will face when writing about her family is determining how much dysfunction is acceptable before it becomes slander. Throw the suggestion of abuse into the mix (that time your mom got drunk and slapped you in front of your friends at your slumber party), and the writer now finds herself having to decide between the truth of her *life* or her *story*.

While mapping the outline of my first book, *Nowhere Near Normal: A Memoir of OCD*, the question of physical abuse wasn't much of a question since it played an extremely small role in my childhood. And with a subtitle like *A Memoir of OCD*, it was easy to assume my readers would understand this was going to be a biography about the kind of trauma you can't cover with concealer and face powder: girl who eats cat food and cannot deal with uneven numbers, raised by a nervous, single working mother, gets sent to live in the family-owned nursing home. Pretty clearcut. Emotional affliction was the focal point of my story.

But here's the thing: A memoir about a crappy childhood is *always* a memoir about a crappy family. There's just no way around it. Whether it be the turmoil of a nomadic childhood (Jeannette Walls's *The Glass Castle*) or the social impact of never having a family to call your own (Antwone Fisher's *Finding Fish: A Memoir*), there's going to come a time when telling your story means thinking about authenticity, and like it or not, the authentic voice of the memoirist requires a certain amount of tattling on the people who have made you what you are.

It was my agent who first brought this to my attention while reading my chapter summaries about growing up with undiagnosed obsessive-compulsive disorder and how it affected those around me. "You've got the *you* part down," she told me, "but I think you're hiding something deeper. If I were a reader, I would feel cheated out of the big picture." I got it. She wanted me to dish, but I wasn't certain I was clever enough to work my way around family psychosis without becoming a narc. After all, wasn't this supposed to be *my* story? I didn't want to turn a book about my mental issues into a drama about my father's outrageous temper or my mother's addiction to pills. When I asked my agent how much of my family's dysfunction I should write about, her advice on the subject of abuse was simply: *"Get it all down."*

"Don't try to compete with Dave Pelzer," she told me—the best-selling author of *A Child Called "It": One Child's Courage to Survive*. "No one had it harder than Pelzer. Your story doesn't even register on the Pelzer scale." But she also advised against adding snippets of abuse if they didn't truly pertain to my story. "Readers are smart," she said. "They'll know when you're hiding something and when you're tacking something on just for effect."

So I thought a lot about abuse. From both sides. I thought about the ways my family suffered while trying to raise a difficult child with an undiagnosed mental illness. I thought about my father and how the stress of our tangled lives played an important role in the way he handled things. The conclusion I came to was this: In order to correctly outline the complexities of how a mentally ill child can destabilize an already-fragile family bond, I would have to write about some things I didn't think were that big of a deal, because they were things my readers would have to know if I wanted my story to be authentic.

My mother and grandmother had passed away over two decades ago, and my sister died from cancer the year before my book was released. As far as hurt feelings and slander were concerned, there simply was no one left to be concerned about.

But when I sent an advance copy to my father, I had no idea my efforts to be so careful would prove to be ineffective. Though almost every scene concerning my father is layered in humorous intent—for example, his single disco days as the only white man in our neighborhood with a full-on afro—ultimately it would be a few short sentences that would turn the truth I told into the truth my father read. I had no idea these two things would never be one and the same.

> Last week my sister got caught riding on the back of some guy's motorcycle, and I saw my father hit her closed-fist in the mouth. When I closed my eyes that night, all I could see was the pink meat of her bottom lip and how her chin was so quickly covered in blood as she ran into the living room.

Those words would be the focal point of every argument and eventually an estrangement.

"How dare you say I was an abusive father," he told me on the phone. I was shocked and confused. A 319-page book, most of it portraying my dad as a hardworking and funny man in the throes of a midlife crisis, and he interprets this one line as me calling him abusive? I tried explaining to him that not a single reviewer even picked up on that; they loved instead the stuff about his red spandex pants and how he would pick me up from school in his Corvette. "Those were some of the highlights that actually sold the book," I said, reminding him that my agent had even suggested I write an entire chapter on the subject of my father's quirkiness, which I did. But none of that mattered. That one little sentence was all he could see, and it would be the catalyst for a long year of tension and fights. At a book release party, he barely spoke to me and instead went around telling the guests, "Don't believe what she says about me." Even though they laughed at his allegation and said they loved what I wrote about him (one man even went out of his way to find my father and tell him he thought the comparison I had made to George Jefferson was hysterical), it wasn't enough. I was hurt and felt terribly misunderstood. I had toiled and wrestled over all the things I wanted to say and how I wanted to say them. I had spent hours writing and rewriting scenes that would create a tribute to our family dynamics. What I felt was that I had created a giant mess.

When I wrote to a friend and fellow memoirist about what my father said and asked her what I should do about it, her response was illuminating. "There's nothing you can do," she told me. "Welcome to the world of memoir."

***

One of the most important things to remember, especially when writing about family, is that your truth is just that—*your* truth. The fight your brother remembers between your parents may involve a fist slamming through a wall in his version, while your memory of that same argument may include your mother locking herself in the bedroom and calling the police. Maybe all of these things happened. Maybe only some of them did. But the memoirist has every right to own her story from *her own* memories. In fact, she has no other choice.

There's a scene in *Nowhere Near Normal*, just after my mother died, where my sister is getting upset about having to pack up the things in our home while I'm making jokes about how we are going to divide up her pills. The universal truth of that day—that scene—is that our mother died at the age of forty-one. And had my sister been alive to read that, as sensitive and close to our mother as she was, there is no way she would have found that scene funny. There isn't a more skilled writer that can make that day un-sad. But my truth of how those events unfolded is very different from my sister's truth, only because the scene is written from my perspective, from the way I handled things, which was to cover hardships with weird jokes. Ironically enough, this is something I inherited from my father. Of course there is nothing truly funny about abuse or death or mental illness, but that's one of the great things about memoirs. When we work it out on the page, we work it out in our own voice and in our truth. I thought that is what I had done. According to my father, I was wrong.

It's almost impossible to make major story changes weeks after an advance copy comes out. When I asked my editor if I should change the line about my father hitting my sister and a few other scenes where I talk about my dad's obsession with women, her answer was clear: "Your job is to tell the story of how your mental illness affected your family. That is the book we bought," she said. "And that's exactly what you did."

Then why did I feel so crummy? Is it because all writers need validation and they need it from just about everyone? I would have given anything to have my father pick up the phone and say, "You did good, and I'm proud of you." Truth telling in memoir is a constant battle of uncertainty, a subjective burden that we can never be sure we are carrying right. I had struggled so much with what to say and what not to say, but my father didn't know this. He didn't know that I'd made choices to protect him or at least choices I'd *thought* would protect him. Didn't I deserve some sort of gratitude for that?

The answer is *no*. When you write about other people, don't expect a thank-you for the things you leave out. You will never get it.

It's been over two years since I last spoke to my father. It's strange to think that the thing I wanted most, to be an author, is the thing that ended our relationship.

When I teach memoir-writing workshops and I share this story, I am asked the question: "Would you go back and take that line out?" When my anger and hurt about his abandonment for telling my truth was ripe, I said, "I should have put in *more* things about his abuse." But now I think I might also answer the question in another way. Now that my memoir is three years behind me, I'm just a daughter who misses her dad, who gets on Facebook to look at pictures of the man who helped give me that story, to see that he is getting old and to wish things would have turned out differently. Both the writer and daughter have good points, but separating the memoir from the memoirist is the one sure path to never again owning the freedom to tell your story, and each of us has that right. Even if—maybe especially if—the truth gets in the way.

Traci Foust is the author of the acclaimed memoir *Nowhere Near Normal*, (Simon and Schuster/Gallery Books, 2011). She has been published in *The Southern Review*, *Emrys Journal*, and *The Nervous Breakdown*, and has won the Northern California Olympiad of the Arts award. Her reviews and interviews have been featured on *Today*, *NPR*, and in *Marie Claire*. She is a regular contributor for the online magazine *Role Reboot*, and a new essay appears in the anthology *SPENT: Exposing Our Complicated Relationship with Shopping* (Seal Press, 2014). She is the mother of four boys and lives in California.

AN ESSAY OPENED THE DOOR TO COMMUNICATION WITH MY DAD
Zoe Zolbrod

When allegations that Woody Allen sexually abused his daughter Dylan Farrow resurfaced, I knew that I wanted to write about it.

For the past few years, I'd been working on a memoir that centers around my own childhood sexual molestation, and I'd done a lot of research on the topic. I thought I had something to say about how we as a culture were responding to the accusations against a celebrity.

A website I'd written for accepted my pitch, but the essay didn't come easily. I wrestled with it for a couple of weeks, working on it and working on it but never quite getting it to crystallize. Finally, the day before the deadline, I rewrote the first half of it in a swoop. I deleted a discussion of celebrity and gossip, and instead I told the story of my own molestation very directly—including that the relative who molested me was sent to prison over twenty-five years later for molesting another little girl, and that until the verdict I had not been entirely clear that what was done to me was horribly wrong.

Although I had been writing a memoir detailing all of this and was at the stage of seeking publication, it turned out that I was more nervous to speak these facts publicly than I had acknowledged to myself. I felt urgent and anxious about the essay appearing, and the night before it was to run, I steeled myself—for what, exactly, I wasn't quite sure. I had vague worries that someone would claim I was lying, that family members would be upset with me, that friends and acquaintances would view me differently, and that I would be yelled at by Internet trolls. I think I was also secretly worried that nothing much at all would happen—that I would find myself dangling far out on a limb and no one would notice. That is the sensation I had in my twenties when I first told my parents about the molestation; the memory of dropping a bombshell and not having it go off remained vivid.

My concerns did not manifest. Instead I started getting a very positive response from the essay within an hour of its going online. The story got picked up by a bigger venue, and tens of thousands of people read it. I was deluged with messages of admiration and support. I received attention for my memoir manuscript from agents and an editor. And I was able to have a better conversation with my father about the events of my childhood than we had ever previously managed.

The guy who had molested me is my father's nephew, who came to live with us as a teenager when I was small. As an adult I started to glean some of the backstory that explained how he had ended up in our house and why my father was particularly concerned about him, but the subject always felt veiled and threatening to me. My father and I are generally close, and I admire him enormously. He's been supportive about everything I've embarked upon, including the writing of a memoir about a difficult subject, in which he is a key figure. Yet we've had a hard time talking about my cousin, what he did to me, and why he ended up in prison.

But my dad and I are both readers and writers, and it's probably fair to say that we find it easier to engage with messy things on the page. Reading my essay prompted my father to investigate some painful chapters of his own life in a way that my sputtering and awkward attempts at conversation never could. He told me that he found himself revisiting the past as well as talking about the causes and effects of child sexual abuse with colleagues who had some experience with it. He acknowledged that he'd been in denial about the issue the first time I brought it up in my twenties. And he set to work writing an essay of his own about the impact my experience had had on him. He generously shared that essay with me before submitting it; I had not given him that same courtesy with my essay or my memoir, but that's all right. I know he understands.

A writer friend of mine likes to say that we write about the things we can't talk about within our families. There's a high value placed on talking through issues in this culture, but sometimes the writing—and reading—can be even more meaningful. I'm acquainted with enough autobiographical writers to know that things don't always work out as sweetly as they seem to have between me and my father right now. But it can happen.

Zoe Zolbrod's forthcoming memoir, *What to Tell*, explores how child sexual abuse reverberates throughout generations of a family. Her first novel, *Currency*, received a Nobbie Award and was a Friends of American Writers prize finalist. Her writing can be found online at *The Rumpus, The Nervous Breakdown, The Weeklings*, and *Salon*. She lives in Evanston, Illinois, with her husband and two children.

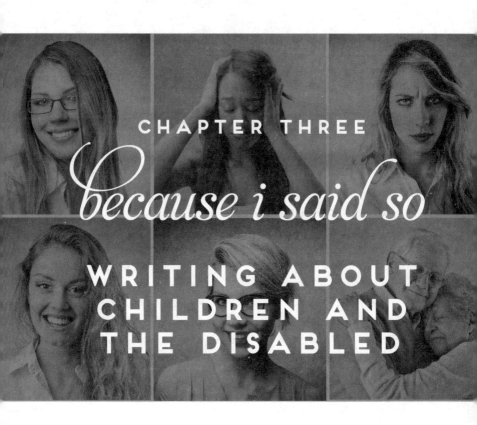

CHAPTER THREE

because i said so

WRITING ABOUT
CHILDREN AND
THE DISABLED

"Writing is a struggle against silence."
—CARLOS FUENTES

The story I wrote about my son in *Seeing Ezra* was perhaps the hardest one I've ever written. I doubt anything will ever be as hard as looking my feelings about him squarely in the face. This is because there are no relationships in the world that are more sacred, that I feel more responsibility for, than the ones with my children.

The danger of writing about our children seems obvious. We conceived them, adopted them, or bonded with them in a blended family. In the beginning, their very survival depends on us. We're responsible for helping them find their sense of self, discover their capabilities, and navigate their young lives. It falls on us to keep them safe and nurtured. Sometimes I feel bad for my children for being born to a memoirist. Sometimes I feel bad for everyone whom I come to love or hate, or who affects me in some way, because they, too, may wind up in one of my books. How is this fair, especially to our dear children? And if the child has a disability, as is the case with my son, the issue of justice seems unbearable. The culture of autism is already riddled with unautistic people speaking for autistic people. Am I just another of many voices drowning out my son's?

Writing about our children and disabled friends or family is a particularly tricky task because we are writing for people who might not be able to speak for themselves, at least not now and at least not in this way. Add to this all the messy societal misconceptions about disability—and even children. It's important to understand how these societal tendencies affect our perceptions of these people in our lives and in our writing. There is a high potential for polemic responses to the author regarding the specific cultural discourses about this subject matter.

To go back to my experience with writing *Seeing Ezra*, I wrote about raising my child in a social climate that stigmatized autism. In the memoir I examined some of the scarier, more difficult feelings I didn't want to admit: the grief I felt over finding out my child wasn't typical, my anger with professionals who misjudged him, and my fury with a culture that didn't welcome my son, that denied he was as important as typical children were. And, then, the grief about that as well.

YOUR STORY OR THEIR STORY

Should I tell this story? You first must determine whose story you're trying to tell. Let me give you a hint: You're writing *your* story. No matter who else you're writing about (your child, a disabled family member or friend) or what the subject matter might be (autism or parenting), a memoir must be about you. These are *your* memories, *your* experiences. The bottom line is that unless you decide to switch to biography or journalism, you can't possibly write about someone else and still call it nonfiction. Note how Christy Shake, author of the blog at www. christyshake.com, writes about her son, who has epilepsy.

> I write in an effort to help me cope with the challenges that I face raising a disabled child. I write [to have] a creative outlet. I write to promote epilepsy awareness, and I'd like to believe that Calvin would appreciate my efforts, my candor, and the raw emotion that I share with the world. I'd like to think he'd "get it."

Shake emphasizes that writing raises awareness and helps her cope. She doesn't try to fill in the blanks about what Calvin might be thinking but instead admits to her audience the same thing she has to admit to herself: It isn't possible for her to know. It's this uncertainty, *her* uncertainty, that becomes her writing's focus.

Jillian Lauren has faced similar challenges to Shake's while working on her second memoir. She says:

> When writing about my son, particularly around the subject of his adoption background, I try to distinguish between what is my story and what is his story. I feel that I can ethically write my story, as fully and truthfully as possible. Those elements of the narrative that are his alone, I keep private. That is a story for him to tell one day or not, as he sees fit.

Lauren clarifies here how important it is to separate her story from her son's. The inclination to tell your child's (or someone else's) story might be compelling for a number of reasons.

- As an attempt to justify your or their actions
- As an attempt to clarify what your child (or someone else) means, for fear that the audience will misinterpret them. (Note: It might

be okay to interpret what you thought they meant, but don't suggest you know what it's like to be them or have their thoughts.)

- As a case of misplaced focus: In other words, maybe you're focusing too much on defending them or taking them too far outside the story.

How do you avoid making these mistakes? Write mindfully. Revise mindfully. Consider carefully the way you're portraying your subject and your relationship to him or her.

Writing about your children or disabled friends and family in memoirs is tricky. You risk being misinterpreted or criticized. You risk pissing off people, harming your reputation, or even losing your job. These risks are inevitable. But sometimes the story you have to tell about your daughter, your son, your friend with brain damage, or your sister with Down syndrome is more important to the world than the chance that you might get criticized. Sometimes your experience can show others something about being human, about living in a difficult world, that they need as badly as you do.

HOW TO WRITE ABOUT CHILDREN AND THE DISABLED

Again, let me be clear: You don't write about children or the disabled in a memoir; you write about yourself. This is key. Claire Dederer wrote the following about her memoir *Poser: My Life in Twenty-Three Yoga Poses*.

> My memoir is about being a mom, but I actually wrote very, very little about my children in the book. I felt that in telling my story of motherhood, there was no need for me to co-opt their experience of growing up. I had no such scruples or hesitations about the adults who appear in my book, but it seemed somehow terribly unfair to write at length about my kids and their natures/characters/

personalities. Identity is hardly fixed for children, and it seemed a horrible responsibility to capture and pin it on their behalf. One reviewer said that the children were the flattest characters in the book, and I took that as a sign that I'd succeeded in writing a book about being a mother but not a book about my children.

In this way, Dederer protects her children's unfolding stories. How you choose to write about them, how much you choose to reveal about your children, will affect others' understandings of who those children are and who they might become, so consider their feelings. You only need to reveal enough about your children or the disabled person in your story to elucidate your own story. Be protective of those who are defenseless. Balance your responsibility to them and your need to tell the truth.

In her memoir *Live Through This: A Mother's Memoir of Runaway Daughters and Reclaimed Love*, Debra Gwartney tells the story of her failed marriage and her move to Eugene, Oregon, with her four daughters, in an attempt to make a fresh start. After the move, her two oldest daughters, who blamed her for the divorce, run away. Gwartney explains her writing process below.

> My daughters would be characters in such an exploration, obviously, but I was charged with largely leaving alone my daughters' interior thoughts, their growth, their insights. My job was to resist pitting us against one another on the page in a way that made me the good guy and to avoid angles of the story that rightly belong to the girls. It was up to me to discover instead what our conflagration had finally taught me about myself.

Gwartney's solution for this problem was to think of her daughters as characters in *her* story. Like all characters in well-written stories, she had to afford them empathy and compassion. She had to develop their characters. But she could not have them share her role as protagonist.

In Molly McCloskey's memoir, *Circles Around the Sun: In Search of a Lost Brother*, she tries to understand who her schizophrenic brother might be. She writes with such precision and honesty that the reader trusts her as she portrays *her* journey in that understanding. Often she offers details that could only be known by someone close to a person with such a severe mental illness. For example, she ponders the fact that her brother has a sort of arrogance to him, that he seems to believe somewhere inside himself that he is superior to others, and that she sees this often with people with schizophrenia. We trust her with these insights because she uses the form of memoir to facilitate her own understanding of who he is, and as a result we come to understand him as well.

HOLDING GRUDGES

Memoir is not a platform to express a grudge. I spent a long time frustrated with the mainstream approach to autism, and I felt furious when the media repeatedly cast autism in a tragic light. It would have been easy to spend time in my memoir garnering sympathy for my plight. A therapist's office is a good place for that. Friends can support you and lend a sympathetic ear. But memoir is, above all else, art. It is art that aims to get at the experience of being human. It is not a place to act out grudges or to go on personal crusades.

Just like all memoirs, the story you have to tell here is about more than just "what happened." It's about your relationship to what happened. Debra Gwartney said once that all memoirs answer the question, "How did I cope?" Certainly that's the case when writing about something difficult we went through with our children. I like to tell students of memoir that the narrator is not "you," the author. The narrator is also not the "you" on the page. It's the *relationship* between the "you" who is writing and the "you" on the page.

Finally, keep in mind that you can't and don't need to tell everything. So many of us have stories that would embarrass us. It's one thing to embarrass ourselves, but is it necessary to potentially embarrass others?

Consider whether such details are essential to your story. Consider, in other words, what it would be like for the person you're writing about if he read the memoir someday. Christy Shake offers the following insights.

> Calvin cannot speak. He cannot walk unassisted; we suppose partly because of his malformed brain, partly due to the seizures it endures, and partly due to the powerful anticonvulsant drugs I must spoon into him every morning, noon, and night. He'll never be able to read or write or understand complex abstract thoughts or ideas. I'll never know his deepest thoughts, perhaps will never know what pains him, vexes him, or frustrates him at any given time. As a result, Calvin will never read what I write about him, although I'd like to think that, if he could, he'd be agreeable.

Todd Drezner, whose documentary *Loving Lampposts: Living Autistic*, is about his autistic son, Sam, feels similarly.

> It occurred to me that Sam was unable to consent to his appearance in the film. At three years old, he didn't understand what the film was about (and he still does not at age nine). He liked watching videos of himself at lampposts in the park, but beyond that, he knew nothing about autism or the controversies surrounding it.

It's essential to think long and hard about which events and situations you'll include in your book. In *Seeing Ezra*, I included a section about Ezra smearing his feces when he was two and three years old. I included this unpleasant memory in order to show just how difficult the parenting situation became for Ezra's father and me. Ezra's poop smearing epitomized the ways in which I didn't understand him and my intense fear for his future, for whether he would be okay in the world someday. But to this day, I worry about having included it. In a panel about writing about our children, Ben Tanzer, author of *Lost in Space: A Father's Journey There and Back Again,* a series of essays about fatherhood, said, "I don't write anything I know my son wouldn't want to be out there." What if, when Ezra is grown, he reads the book and feels embarrassed? What if a friend reads it and judges him in some way? I may never know if I made the right decision.

WHAT TO EXPECT WHEN WRITING ABOUT YOUR CHILDREN AND THE DISABLED

When *Seeing Ezra* came out, I was terrified. It was one thing to hear people's criticism about my relationships with my parents and men. It's quite another to hear people's problems with my relationship with my child. If there's anything I'm tender about, it's my parenting, surely because it's the thing in my life I'm least secure about doing well. Luckily for me, almost all of the reviews were good. Many parents reached out to me to let me know how much the book meant to them as fellow parents of autistic children. A couple reviews were not as good. They criticized the book for showing too much anger about the services we received for Ezra and how ineffective they can be. No one, thank goodness, suggested that I was a bad mother or that Ezra was anything other than lovable.

Lynn Beisner had a much more frightening experience.

> Primarily I have written about myself and my family. I have had a lot of concerns about writing about them. The first and primary one is for their safety. A couple of years before I began writing professionally, I wrote a piece that dealt with my experience of being a whistleblower in a case of clergy sexual abuse of children. I received personal death threats (expected), but what … frightened me beyond words was that I received a very

graphic threat to my daughter, calling her by name and mentioning the school that she attended. To put the threat in polite and printable language, [the person] ... threatened to rape my daughter with a shotgun and then end her life by discharging the gun within her vagina. When I brought it to the attention of our local law enforcement, they literally laughed and said that I should be glad [we were] ... only threatened. Writing like mine had been known to incite violence. It was eerily similar to how rape victims are often blamed for the crime committed against them. [The experience] gave me a small glimpse of what I could expect should a member of my family or I be injured because of something that I wrote.

Of course I wanted to protect my family's privacy. I was especially concerned about sharing things about my children's lives. I discussed with each child what I might want to share, and the nonessential elements of the story that we could change so as not to accidentally reveal anyone's identity.

So much about the repercussions of writing remains beyond our control. People's responses can be shocking and unexpected, and there's no way to prepare for them. At the same time, for every negative response, there will be many more positive ones, which Beisner also notes.

I am surprised by how many e-mails and messages ... I get from people who tell me that my writing has in some way eased their pain. And at the end of the day, there is only one reason to do something as difficult, painful, and revealing as memoir writing, and that is because you want to ease or to prevent the suffering of others.

Susan Senator shares an unexpected effect of writing about her autistic son.

> I did like how writing about these very emotional events helped me make more sense of a very difficult time (the early years of motherhood with an autistic firstborn son). I only regret having been so sad while I was raising them. Once those days are gone, they are gone. I wish I could have enjoyed them more.

Although Susan can't get those years back, she found sense in them through her writing. Grief and regret can be terrible feelings when suffered alone. By capturing them on the page and sharing them with her readers, many who feel the same way, she healed one of her wounds. She worked through feelings that she may not have been able to sort out in any other way. Perhaps even more powerful, she engaged with others in order to do so.

Memoir provides a connection between the writer and reader. A sort of intimacy is forged when someone reads your book and both you *and* your reader wind up less alone in the world. If parenting is lonely, if loving someone with a disability is isolating, memoir can bridge that divide between you and everyone else who feels the way you do.

EXERCISES

1. Write a scene consisting of a particularly difficult interaction between you and your child or between you and a disabled person in your memoir. What were your feelings surrounding this interaction? Did you feel embarrassed? Protective? How do these feelings speak to your awareness of others' reactions to these individuals?

2. Make a list of emotions that describe your relationship with a child or a disabled person in your memoir. Are there emotions you're ashamed of or embarrassed about? Write a scene where you are forced to confront these emotions in some way.

3. Write a scene in your memoir from the perspective of someone entirely outside your relationship with the child or disabled person from the last exercise, such as a stranger or acquaintance. What happens to the scene when it is skewed toward someone else's reality? What insights are lost when the perspective shifts from parent/caretaker to someone outside of this relationship?

4. Pick a memoir that focuses on the author's relationship with children or the disabled. What do you notice about how the author dealt with their relationships with these characters? In what ways does the author's identity evolve as a result of his experiences with these characters? Which aspects of the memoir would you include in your own work? Which aspects would you change? How so?

5. Pick a memoir that focuses on the author's relationship with children or the disabled. Consider any unique family situations, traits, or beliefs that affected the author's experience as a parent or caretaker. Did she have a sibling or several siblings with a similar condition? Was she raised with certain beliefs about raising children or caring for the disabled? What unique circumstances are important to your memoir? How do these circumstances help you communicate your experience to your readers?

SEE DICK WRITE
Ben Tanzer

I wasn't raised with many rules.

I had to call home by midnight. And no young women were allowed to get pregnant in the house.

Those were the biggies.

There were unwritten rules, too, of course. You must take care of yourself, be that getting to school on your own, doing the laundry, dealing with injuries, or what have you. You must move away from home, be curious, and see the world. You must be a voice for the oppressed.

Also, you must not be a dick.

That last one may be a self-defined rule born of the others. Still, it is a good rule, and I hope to pass it along to my children as well.

The fact remains, though, that despite, or is it in spite of, all this, I was and remain rule bound.

But what does that mean?

It means that I need to check my alarm and the lock on the door repeatedly before I go to sleep. That the laundry has to be folded in the laundry room—you can't just cram it into the laundry basket and carry it upstairs. And then after that, it has to be properly refolded neatly and placed in piles.

On the other hand, I try not to have any rules about writing: nothing precious, no perfect time of day or place, no need for the right kind of coffee or music. The light doesn't have to be right either, and I never wait for inspiration or a manic burst of ideas to get started. Further, I don't have to write a set number of words. When I'm done, I'm done.

However, I do have to sit down and write for a thirty-minute block every day. And it can't be twenty-eight minutes either; it can't be close. It has to be at least thirty minutes. Further, those thirty minutes can include editing but not research, and it's not that research isn't cool; I love research. It's just that research must occur outside of that thirty-minute block.

Which, to point out the obvious, is sort of a rule I guess, which brings us to parenting, because parenting is all about making rules and all about breaking them.

So in terms of my parenting rules, there are these: I will not yell at my child. I will not mess with nap-time. I will always use a car seat. I will enforce time-outs. I will not give in to whining. I will make time to take care of myself and my other relationships. I will not lie to my children or myself about my children. I will not let them sit in front of a screen if they don't do their homework, take a shower, put away the laundry, and on and on. I will not make so many rules. And I will not be a dick.

Of course I have and continue to break all of those rules all of the time; it's impossible not to, and I accept that.

Which brings us to the subject of writing about my children (Myles, twelve, and Noah, eight), which I have done in writing my dad-centric essay collection, *Lost in Space*. I had to have rules to do this. Not many, mind you, but not none, either.

And I couldn't break them, or I tried not to, anyway.

First, no stories or threads about anything they considered a secret of theirs, which would not be cool, and so if it felt like a secret of theirs, it was off-limits.

Embarrassment is a different matter, however.

So for example, writing about my sex talk with Myles as I did in the essay "Bed Sex" seemed like fair game. He may or may not be embarrassed about this piece at fifteen, and he may very well find it funny at twenty-five or at his wedding rehearsal.

We don't know, but there are no secrets in this case. The piece mostly, and consciously, pokes fun at me. He is a little boy, and his questions are adorable. Meanwhile, my fumbling with women, with this discussion, and the lack of guidance I received about any of it, is the core of the piece.

In fact, I am the main character in all of these pieces, and while that wasn't a rule, it helped in not breaking this first one.

Second, while it would be endlessly easy to write about the parent-related pain and the bitching that is constantly going on in my head, not to mention the incredible rage I sometimes always feel, who the fuck wants to read that book?

No one, and so the individual pieces, where possible, and the collection overall, had to be balanced with humor.

Balance in life, in family, in work, along with somehow balancing one's poor choices with healthier ones, may very well be the key to managing anything, but a book hoping to wallow in the muck and glory of parenting begs for it.

Hence, a piece like the title essay, "Lost in Space," where my wife and I were worried that Noah's spine might not descend on its own, required that I also write about Myles covering the house in vomit the night before Noah's MRI, because that is parenting, which is often simultaneously funny and horrible.

Further, I had to describe how I questioned whether the resident working on Noah's case was withholding the results of said MRI because he was so fucking handsome, and attractive people feel they can do whatever the fuck they want because no one ever calls them on their shit.

I also had to question my desire to punch him in the face, which is less funny, I suppose, but I really do have a lot of rage, and why hide from that?

The third rule: There should be no repetition of a single theme in the collection, which in this case meant recognizing that anyone writing about parenting can write about the trauma of letting go of their child, the endless touchstones and the moments where we realize just how necessary it all is, crushing, yet inevitable. But how many times does anyone want to read about it?

Case in point, years ago I wrote about Myles's first haircut and the incredible torture I felt at the act of cutting his beautiful, scraggly, rock-star tendrils in a piece I titled "The Boy with the Curious Hair."

At the time, I rarely wrote about him, and that act of watching his hair fall away and reveal his no-longer-baby face prompted a true rumination on letting him go.

Revisiting that piece now, though, in the context of all the pieces in *Lost in Space*, it wasn't going to fly as originally conceived.

Instead it became a piece focused on whether cutting his hair might possibly undermine his potential Samson-like powers and his chance to be a superhero, while also exploring and making peace with the idea that even if any of that was possible, wouldn't a child who might grow to be curious, caring, a voice for the oppressed, and so not a dick, be just as heroic as an actual superhero might be?

The final rule of thumb was based on a discussion with my editor.

Is *Lost in Space* a collection of essays about a writer who is a father, writing about wherever he was on the path to becoming a father, whether he was thinking about becoming a father or not? Or did these essays require that my "dad filter" exist at all times, wherever I was on the journey?

For example, when I first wrote "The Unexamined Life," I was a guy with a newly dead father who hoped to someday soon be a father himself, and I decided to go backpack across Italy as I contemplated those things.

But now I am that father. So what has more value as a writer: falling in love with Michelangelo's *David* as a wandering traveler who happened to know he would eventually get home and hope to have a child, or falling in love with Michelangelo's *David* but also wondering how my still-unborn children would someday react to *David* themselves?

I went with the latter.

Is the essay better now? Not necessarily. But is the collection more cohesive? Indeed it is.

None of which speaks to how my children might react to the collection when they finally read it, which is something I've thought about when Myles asks, "Why can't we read it? It's about us; isn't it?"

Well, yes and no.

It's really about me, and do they need to know at this early age how fucked I am? Not really. However, do I want to respect and encourage their curiosity? I do.

So I asked Myles if he wanted to read "The Boy with the Curious Hair," but thus far he hasn't accepted the invitation. I'm not sure why this is, and he isn't saying, but I suspect he has rules about such things.

Ben Tanzer is the author of the books *My Father's House; You Can Make Him Like You; Lost in Space* (found at www.curbside splendor.com/curbside/books/lost-in-space); *Four Fathers*, which he co-authored with Dave Housley, BL Pawelek, and Tom Williams; and *Orphans*, which won the 24th Annual Midwest Book Award in Fantasy/Science Fiction/Horror/Paranormal, among others. He also directs publicity and content strategy for Curbside Splendor and can be found online at *This Blog Will Change Your Life* (bentanzer. blogspot.com), the center of his vast, albeit faux, lifestyle empire.

CONVERSATIONS
Carolyn Roy-Bornstein

I am not one of those parents who have been writing about their children since they were born. I was a nurse when my boys were little. I became a doctor when they were six and eight. I didn't have time to write. I barely kept up with their baby books, capturing even fewer cute stories about my second child than I did about my first. Other writers I know who have written about their kids agonized over it. "Do I change their names? Change *mine*? Will they hate me when they're grown?"

I only started writing about my children after my seventeen-year-old was hit by a drunk driver in a crash that killed his girl-friend, Trista, and left him with a serious traumatic brain injury. Even then, it took me five years to get the first word down. At first, it was all I could do to keep putting one foot in front of the other.

Neil spent a week in the intensive-care unit at a major trauma center in Boston, the doctors performing CAT scan after CAT scan, trying to decide if the bleeding in his brain was going to stop or require surgery. He spent months in physical therapy learning to walk on a newly nailed-together leg. He spent years on antide-pressants and in therapy, his depression caused as much by his brain injury as by the loss of Trista. What should have been the time of his life—senior year of high school—was one long struggle. My boy, who got a perfect 800 on his math SATs, now needed academic accommodations just to graduate. College was equally disastrous. My once gregarious son now hung back in crowds, his memory loss preventing him from distinguishing between kids whose names he should know from those he'd never met. He lacked confidence. Friends scattered, unsure of how to respond to this new Neil.

While initially it was all I could do to take care of Neil, eventually I felt a deep need to understand what our family had just been through together. And I began to write. Sure, I had journaled all the way through Neil's ordeal. From his bedside, I captured every IV line inserted, every blood draw endured. But it wasn't until five years after the crash that I really let myself explore my feelings on the page. I wrote articles for disability journals sharing our experience of coping with the accident's aftermath. I wrote essays in medical journals about grappling with whether and how to share my family's experience with my patients. I wrote essays for literary anthologies on journaling through sorrow. Finally I wrote and published a full memoir about the trauma our family went through. *Crash: A Mother, a Son, and the Journey from Grief to Gratitude* limned the fine balance between the gratitude I felt because my son survived the crash and the grief I experienced over everything he had lost.

I have never published a word about Neil without him reading it first. I would never be comfortable with my words about him being out in the world if he had not read and approved each one. It became more important to me as the publications became more numerous and had larger circulations. An essay in a medical or rehabilitation journal was only going to be read by medical folks like me. The literary magazines in which my work about Neil first appeared were followed largely by moms. None of Neil's friends were likely to stumble upon any of them. But *The Boston Globe* was a bigger deal. It was critical to me that he knew exactly what I was writing and exactly where each story appeared.

The memoir was different from any of that. There would be a book launch in town. His friends *would* read it. (Or at least their moms would.) So as I wrote, I sent him each chapter and asked for feedback. And he gave it. At first he made minor, less-than-relevant corrections. "My graduation robe was maroon, Mom, not black." Or he would make random suggestions on seeming minutiae. "I don't think you should use the word *tertiary*, Mom. I don't think most people will know what *tertiary* means." But that wasn't what I wanted from him. I wanted to know how it made him feel—how it *would* make him feel if his friends read the book. I wanted to know if I was capturing his experience accurately and if not, where I had gone wrong.

One day, though, Neil gave me more than just feedback on my writing. He told me how he felt. I had e-mailed him a chapter about how now, ten years after the crash, his dad and I sometimes still don't know what to make of him. By that I mean we sometimes look at him and wonder if what we are seeing—the stony silence, the awkward pause—is a result of his brain injury or if this is just who Neil is now, who he would have become without the trauma.

That night the phone rang. It was Neil, an unusual call, as he's not much of a phone guy. He got right to the point.

"You know that part in the book where you wonder if it's the brain injury you're looking at or if it's just me?"

"Yes."

"Well ..."

And here was one of those long pauses that made me wonder. I held my breath.

"... I wonder that sometimes myself."

I let my breath out. He went on to say that he's come to understand that it doesn't really matter how he got here. "It's just who I am right now." I don't know if this was the result of his many years of therapy since the crash or if he had come to this realization himself, but it didn't matter. He had given me insight into his world. And my book had given us a way to talk about an event that had happened ten years ago, the conversations about it long gone cold.

One day not long ago, he called me up and asked if I could send him copies of his CAT scans and also the results of his neuro-psychological testing.

"Sure, Neil. How come?" I asked.

"I'm petitioning the disabilities office at my school for longer test-taking time and a distraction-free environment."

At the time, Neil was in graduate school and was in a room-mate situation. One of his roommates collected social security, her hip congenitally displaced.

"That's awesome, Neil. Did you get that idea from talking to Starr?"

"No, Mom. I got it from reading your book."

Not only was my book helping us all talk about Neil's brain injury, it was also giving him ideas for how to deal with it. Just as I advocated for him in high school and college ten years prior, now Neil was advocating for himself in graduate school.

Even though I solicited Neil's feedback when I was writing my book, the first time he read my words was not actually with my permission. One day, a few weeks after he was discharged from the hospital, I came home to find him sitting at the dining room table, a book open in front of him. But it wasn't just any book. It was my journal. My heart skipped a beat. What had I written there? I racked my brain: Neil pulling off his hospital gown, Neil lashing out at the hospital staff, Neil needing to be restrained.

But before I could decide whether to ask him to stop reading my private entries or let him continue, he looked up at me, his face blank as a plate.

"I'm sorry I yelled at you in the hospital, Mom."

My heart cracked. Here was my boy apologizing for some-thing totally beyond his control—uninhibited rants caused by his temporal-lobe agitation. He didn't know he had yelled at me. He didn't know anything. He was totally amnesic for his entire stay in the ICU. I squeezed his shoulders and pressed my lips to the top of his head.

I knew at that moment that he needed to recover information about those lost days. My journal was filling in his memory for him. He was learning things from the page that I could not bring myself to express out loud: the breadth and depth of my love for him, my deep sorrow at not being able to take away his pain, my guilt at being the mother of the one who survived this terrible accident, my guilt at feeling guilty.

"It's okay, Neil. Read what you want. I'll be here if you have any questions."

But I hovered as he read. I pretended to dust, flipped through books, all the while keeping a wary eye on my son. I worried about what his reaction would be. Embarrassment at his uncharacteristic behavior in the hospital. Anger at me for writing about it. Finally he closed the back cover of the notebook and looked up at me.

"I just like that song," he finally said.

For weeks after the accident, Neil listened to Trista's favorite band, They Might Be Giants, sing a song called "Dead" every morning in the shower. The irony of that song choice was not lost on me. In my journal I had written that I was worried it might be more than coincidence. I worried that it meant he was stuck, obsessing over his lost girlfriend. But here he was reassuring me that this was not the case. Here we were, reassuring each other that it was okay.

Though sometimes in asking Neil's permission to publish, I simply e-mailed him the copy and waited for the okay, at other times, when things were particularly sensitive, I had him read it in person. I had to be sure he actually read each word. In one piece, I wrote about the doctors testing Neil's hearing in the hospital by rubbing his hairs together in front of his ears and asking him what he heard.

"Beating off," was Neil's reply, a helpful reassurance that his hearing was intact but a startling sign that his frontal lobe was not doing its normal filtering job.

When I asked him whether it was okay to share that, he nodded.

I wrote about Trista's mother, Mary, reading Trista's diary after she died and finding out that Neil and Trista had had sex.

"If Trista were alive, I'd kill Neil," she told me. "But since she's dead, I'm grateful to him for giving her that experience as a woman."

"Can that stay, Neil?" I asked.

Neil caught his breath and blinked as he read, then looked me right in the eye.

"It can stay," he said.

Neil came to my book launch party. He mapped out the timing beforehand: when the actual reading would be, the schmoozing, the food. I was not surprised when he was not in the gathering I greeted when I arrived on the scene. I was not surprised when I did not see his face among those seated in chairs listening to the talk. But after the reading, when the crowd dispersed to eat cake and the line formed to have their books signed, there he was: my stalwart support.

That night, Neil took home a few copies of the book for himself. Since then, he has called me up several times requesting additional books.

"Can I have one for Ari?" he'd ask. "I also need one to send to Jeff."

After the fourth or fifth such request, I began to see a pattern. My book was fulfilling yet another purpose. It was serving as code. As explanation. Neil could hand it to friends who may not have understood what was going on all those years ago. Neil giving them my book and saying, "This is what my mom wrote," was also his way of saying, "This is what it was like for me. This is who I am."

My words have served as many things for our family. In the early days of the accident, my journal was Neil's memory, filling in the time he missed. It has served as an icebreaker, allowing us to once again talk as a family about something that for so long stayed undiscussed, opening some wounds in the process but ultimately allowing for deeper healing. It served as education, helping Neil to not only recognize his limitations but to advocate for himself to get his needs met. Finally, it has been his shorthand, letting friends more deeply into his world.

There is a lot of talk in memoir about this concept of truth, of telling the truth no matter what the fallout. I always gave Neil total veto power over anything I wrote about him. If he had been uncomfortable with my words, I would not have published them. I wouldn't have changed things or lied; I just would have kept particular scenes private at his request. Maybe if I had written this book years ago when he was still a teen, he would have objected. But I couldn't have written it until I did. The writer Graham Greene talks about "the sliver of ice in the heart" of the artist necessary to write about our world. I interpret that to mean that we need temporal distance, rather than detachment, from significant events in order to gain a proper frame of reference to write about them. It's what I teach my writing students who try to write about their divorces even as they are going through them. And while time gives the writer that needed perspective, perhaps it helps the subject, too. To see things as they are. To balance the *what could have been* with the *what is*. To accept another's interpretation of the heart.

Carolyn Roy-Bornstein is a pediatrician whose son suffered a traumatic brain injury in 2003. Her 2012 memoir *Crash: A Mother,* *a Son, and the Journey from Grief to Gratitude* details the experience from her "other side of the stretcher" perspective. Her nonfiction has appeared in the *The Boston Globe, The Writer, JAMA*, the *American Medical Writers Association Journal*, and many other venues. Her story "What Halley Heard" won third place in the 2004 Writer's Digest Short Short Story Competition. Her new book, *Chicken Soup for the Soul, Recovering from Traumatic Brain Injuries: 101 Stories of Hope, Healing, and Hard Work* was released in June 2014.

SKIPPING STONES
Deb Stone

In March 2013, I finished revising *Mother Up: A Memoir,* which is about my transformation from a single mother of twins to an expert foster mom. I understood that my story overlapped with private moments in my family members' lives. How would they handle that?

For nineteen years, I have been a Court Appointed Special Advocate, a "CASA" designated by the judge to be "the eyes and ears of the court" and "the voice of the child" for children in foster care. I learned that reporting adverse information to the Court without telling the parents in advance caused them to feel blindsided. The more negative the narrative, the more important it was to offer the parents an opportunity to process it privately. As I considered my memoir, I thought, *If this is my commitment to strangers, how could I not do it for the people I love?*

I chose several family members to read the manuscript, not offering to change what I'd written—memoir is not collaboration—but to provide each with an opportunity to read what I'd said about them before it went out into the world. I was concerned about my first foster son, Allen, now an adult in his thirties, because I knew my perspective about him as a boy might be painful for him to process. Moreover, I understood that the theme of my memoir, the importance of needing a mother, remained a tender place in many former foster children.

I also knew all these years later that I had failed to understand that my ten-year-old foster son Allen's calls for attention were cries for a mom. Not a foster mom who judged him as a child needing to be saved. Not as a child who needed discipline (although he did), but as a mother who recognized that seventeen prior homes was too many for any child. I was one more woman in a line of women he'd come to know would disappoint him. Nine years later, Allen sat on a barstool in our kitchen, not making eye contact with me as I cooked dinner.

"You weren't the kind of mother I needed," he said.

He'd said it many times. Each time, I tried to convince him that I was a good mom. Wasn't I there for him day in and day out? Hadn't I bought him the trendy shoes and clothes he wanted? Paid for him to go to surf camp? Hadn't I arranged for him to be a boom operator on a feature film? Taken him on a trip to Germany and the Czech Republic? Loaded bags of groceries to take during visits with his birth mother?

Allen brought up my insufficient mothering at various intervals until that particular day—him on the barstool, me standing in the kitchen, the countertop between us, all the years that we'd struggled to live as mother and son between us, all the moments of hurt that I knew and didn't know between us—and it hit me: *Had I been mother enough?* Not on the days he had needed me to be something more.

"I hear you," I said. "I gave you 100 percent of what I had to give. I'm sorry it wasn't enough."

He nodded as if he accepted it. The next time the subject bounced up, he was twenty-nine, and he sent me an e-mail asking why my husband and I had adopted other children but not him: *I just wanted to let you know how I really feel and how confusing it all has been and still is.* It was a hard question, and I sent the best response I could muster. I hoped it would be more satisfying once he read my memoir.

Allen's intelligence has always served as counterweight to his loss and pain. When he was a child, I perceived him as relentless in his challenges. His intellectual prowess always seemed to be about making sure he came out on top. He needed to be important. I mistook that for needing to be number one. He had never been one to show his feelings. And, for me, if I could not see emotion in you, I did not trust you. I had not trusted Allen as a child, and even if I had reasons that were legitimate at the time, Allen had always known it; he had always *felt* it, amidst all the other complicated things he felt and could not say.

By the time I finished the memoir, Allen was thirty. I explained that it might be difficult to read, that he had challenged me in ways no other child had, and that I would be revealing things about him in order to reveal myself. I sent him the manuscript and then worried about how he was managing. I called. He didn't answer. I sent him e-mails and private messages on Facebook. Silence for weeks. Finally, he responded. *I am shocked at how you saw me ... I feel like you never really understood me .... On a personal level, I have distanced myself from most of [my] childhood, and I hardly identify with it anymore.*

If you have parented, you know about guilt.

I thought back to a message he'd sent me a few months earlier: *The only thing I hope you know is that you were the bridge between a very messy, likely very sad, life and whatever this is I have here to-day … [You were there] for many years through many changes … it was not all fishing and heart-to-hearts … but it was the cornerstone.* This was the child I worried for, the boy that carried the weight of my transference (a mucky conglomerate of genuine and mistaken concerns) *in situ* my brother Jimmy. Allen came laden with diagnoses and psychological evaluations, a boy whose history would cause any child to act out in ways adults had labeled as wrong. This was the boy I loved, now a man with the clarity to say, *It's your story, but I appreciate that you might consider how some of that feels to me.*

He was too hurt to meet in person or talk on the phone. For several weeks, we messaged back and forth. I tried to respond to his feelings without defending the point of view I'd taken in my memoir. It was hard to witness him wrangle the feelings that rose up from reading my characterization of him as a boy. We muddled through until he felt heard and understood.

Without the interventions you created, who knows where I'd be now? Maybe in that way, it's a luxury to be able to complain about things … . So in place of "Maybe I was screwed up," I'd submit, without the help I did receive, maybe I would have been much worse. I was often impulsive and did things that I did not always understand. Some of my behaviors were inappropriate for the time. I lied a lot, however, to myself first and then to other people. It was a full-time job that I'm pleased not to have anymore …. People do the best they can … you and me included. We can't go back and change things. …. Reading about myself as a child just struck a [chord] in me. But in some ways I feel fairly neutral about it now.

I didn't need his blessing, but neither did I want to hurt him. He came to me as a child without power or control in his life. The power I could offer him now was the opportunity to read my memoir before it was published. Despite the shock and hurt Allen felt at reading my portrayal of him as a child, he also shared excellent insights about the places I'd held back, such as when he pointed out, *There is no talk about your anger and only one small paragraph about being controlling that seems like more of a cute joke. The first half seems very introspective, full access, and like you came to some kind of inner conclusion. The second half talks about yourself so little it seems like avoidance.* Even in the midst of discussing our difficult experiences, he held up a mirror so that I might see myself more clearly. Those reflections improved the quality of my next revision.

Sharing my memoir with my foster son was meaningful even though it was difficult. His past had been painful, and I was part of that pain. Sharing my manuscript before it was published provided an opportunity for us to share feelings we'd carried for years but hadn't articulated—me, until I wrote the memoir, and him, until he'd read it. On Mother's Day, he brought me a wire basket filled with smooth stones to skip across our pond. Our relationship may bump along at times, born of bonds forged in trauma, but I love this child of mine, this now adult man, and he loves me. We know that better now for having shared our words.

Deb Stone's writing has appeared in *STIR Journal, The Oregonian, Portland Tribune, The Portland Upside,* and *Clackamas Literary Review.* Her essay "Mr. Potato Head's Secret Life" was read at Portland, Oregon's inaugural *Listen to Your Mother* show. Deb has been a Court Appointed Special Advocate for twenty-four neglected and abused kids in foster care, and a foster, step-, adoptive, and birth parent to more than thirty children. She provides training to child advocates, social workers, and parents. She is currently writing the sequel to her memoir *Mother Up.* You can find Deb on social media @iwritedeb or www.debstone.net.

CHAPTER FOUR

dangerous liaisons

WRITING ABOUT SPOUSES, FRIENDS, AND EXES

One of the great ironies of memoir is that while we write about ourselves, we have to write about others. We define ourselves in relation to others. The arc of our stories are interwoven with the people we come to know, whom we come to love, betray, get betrayed by, and lose. In the midst of writing about these people, we risk bringing up unresolved feelings of anger, outrage, and grief—theirs and ours—and that puts all of us on unstable ground.

When writing about your close relationships with lovers and dear friends, perhaps the first question to ask is "What story am I trying to tell?" Jillian Lauren, author of *Some Girls: My Life in a Harem,* explains.

> I examine my intentions very carefully. I ask myself:
> Are you writing this because it's essential to the story?
> Is this a story that has resonance that goes beyond just
> lil' old me? Am I being truthful? Am I coming from a
> perspective of love? If the answer to those things is yes,
> then I go ahead and write it.

Before writing any memoir, we must examine what our intentions are. Memoir must never be a vehicle for revenge or a platform to explain your side of a story. Rather, it must always be a vehicle for truth, compassion, and self-examination. Gigi Little, who wrote and published an essay about her ex-husband, speaks about her desire not to hurt others.

> I think I tend to be overanxious about any writing I do
> about other people, but with [my ex-husband], there's the
> added worry of: I left him; I hurt him; I don't want to
> hurt him again. … My most recent essay, "Shopping with
> Clowns," is about the same time period as [my novel-in-
> progress, which] deals with the same shame I carry for
> having lied to myself—and him—for so long, staying mar-
> ried when I didn't love him. It talks about those same
> traits of his that I know would hurt him to read, how he
> was selfish and shallow and (in some ways, worse) boring.

Little recognizes that writing has the potential to be a sort of weapon, and it is always a memoirist's job to prevent this from happening—or to cause as little harm as possible. This is the question that must hover as you write about exes and the like: How do I write authentically about this person, and how do I also keep him or her safe?

HOW TO WRITE ABOUT EXES, FRIENDS, AND OTHER PEOPLE YOU MIGHT PISS OFF

Gigi Little's concerns about hurting her ex-husband were understandable, but she went on to say why she wrote her essay anyway.

> One of the interesting things to me about my anxious, neurotic self is that when I'm in the act of writing, I'm not thinking about those concerns. It never stops me. I'm thinking about what I want to say and how I want to say it. I'm thinking what's going to make this a good sentence, paragraph, essay, memoir. There's a way I can separate out my writing self from the me who obsesses over it while brushing my teeth or walking the dog. In a way, writing about that story in my life is an extension of that story in my life. That story was about feeling second all the time, feeling not listened to, and I wonder how much my wanting to write about it now is me wanting that chance to be heard.

When we write memoir, we aren't just telling a story about what happened between us and other people. We write our stories in order to solve something, to re-envision a part of our lives. Gigi Little found that the writing fulfilled a need that her relationship never could. Writers know this about writing. The worries, the concerns, the anxiety about that person out in the world are usually unfounded. Or, at the very least, they are unpredictable. You can't know how that person will really feel. You also can't know that the person will even read your piece. I like to tell students that all the worries in the world are wasted anxiety until you've written something. Otherwise you're worrying about something that doesn't exist, that may well never happen. Like Mark Twain once said, "I am an old man and have known a great many troubles, but most of them have never happened."

Okay, so you decide to go ahead and write the memoir. You have to. It won't sleep in your mind. It demands to be written. Now what? Now, you write. You write, and you write, and you write. Don't think about all those concerns during your first draft. But when it comes time for revision, consider the following.

INCLUDE ONLY WHAT'S RELEVANT

Do you need to include the fact that your ex-wife has a wide scar on her inner thigh? Only if that scar plays an important part in your story; for example, if the person she was cheating with told you he knew about that scar. If not, leave that detail out. Writers are often told to include as much concrete detail as possible. Memoir writers are told to give all the facts. But these two pieces of advice aren't as imperative as the human beings we write about, who are at least as important as the writing itself, usually even more so.

CHANGE WHATEVER IDENTIFYING DETAILS YOU CAN

For instance, if your friend works at Intel, why can't she work at Xerox instead? Even better, do you need to note where she works or what she does for a living? I made this mistake in *Loose Girl*. One of my ex-boyfriends was furious because I noted which state he was from, what his interests were, and where he lived now. He told me that people he knew (but who didn't know me or our past together) had read the memoir and knew immediately that those chapters were about him. He felt violated. The bottom line is that he was right. I could just as easily have said he was from Virginia or Montana. I hadn't been careful with his private life. Sue William Silverman, author of *Love Sick: One Woman's Journey Through Sexual Addiction*, shares her story about changing details below.

> In *Love Sick*, I mainly write about nonfamily members, and I wanted to protect the privacy of these people

(which is easier to do than with family). For example, I changed the names of the men with whom I acted out my sexual addiction. Unlike family members, these men, when all is said and done, were rather interchangeable, so I didn't see any need to reveal their true identities. I also changed the names of the women who were with me during rehab to protect their privacy as well. The names of these people didn't matter. I was able to convey my truths regardless. I was, however, a bit concerned about my former husband in terms of *Love Sick*. I called him prior to publication, as I felt he should know that he was included in the book. I reassured him, however, that I changed his name; I also reassured him by letting him know that the focus of the book (of course) was on me and I wasn't revealing any of his secrets. At the time, he seemed fine with this. Nevertheless, I was concerned because while we were married I hadn't revealed the extent of my sexual addiction; however, we were now divorced, so, really, what difference did it make?

SHOW BOTH SIDES OF THE COIN

To quote Cheryl Strayed from chapter two, "… if you're going to show anyone's ass, it better be your own." Whatever happened in your life, you were actively involved. You were at least half responsible. Don't get me wrong; some things are beyond your control—if you were sexually abused, or if you were born into poverty, for instance. Some things *do* just happen to you. But when you write about your relationship with a person, there is a mutuality that must be acknowledged. Nobody wants to hear about what a victim you are. They want to know how you got yourself into a hairy situation and then how you got yourself out. They want to know what you gleaned from your experiences. They want to know how you would not be you, in all your beautiful wonder, if it were not for your time with this person.

Consider what Susan Shapiro wrote in *The New York Times* about taking responsibility for her role in her memoir *Five Men Who Broke My Heart*.

> I was attempting to chronicle my midlife crisis when, as a married forty-year-old journalist, I re-met my top five heartbreaks. I assumed that admitting in public that I'd been dumped five times in the title made me sufficiently pathetic. But early on, I wasn't weak, vulnerable, or relatable. I came across as flippant and cavalier instead of as someone who was hurting; the stakes weren't high enough. In short, I hadn't dug deep enough into my real anxiety.[1]

Gigi Little also had to take a close look at her intentions and feelings when writing about her childhood best friend.

> In my essay, "Shopping with Clowns," I did something I'd never done in writing and had rarely, if ever, done in real life. I said, "I hate her."
>
> Actually, the line is, "I kind of hated her," but the "kind of" was more about voice and less about back-pedaling. She was my best friend from fourth through eighth grade, back when it was so important to have a best friend that it was all right that she pushed you around and made you feel like a bug. I'd always hated her. But now, forty-plus years old and thirty-plus years away from her, I stopped before letting my fingers type the words. Part guilt, part paranoia. Hate was such an ugly thing, and whenever I thought it about anybody,

---

1 opinionator.blogs.nytimes.com/2012/12/31/make-me-worry-youre-not-o-k

half of me was half-sure that person could hear into my brain.

Okay, I kind of loved it, too. The thought of making that statement and putting it out into the world. The thought of getting a bit snarky on the page about this prissy, patronizing bully of a best friend who'd probably never even buy the book and know I'd written this anyway, right? Right?

I have to say, what a release [it was] when I typed those words. It occurred to me as I wrote, "I kind of hated her," that I deserved to be able to say it. And I deserved to feel it. I don't know why that never really occurred to me before. And it occurred to me that if she did read my essay and if she contacted me and told me what she thought of me because of what I'd said, I deserved to say to her [that] it was the truth.

Little recognizes how important it is to differentiate in memoir between who a person is and how you feel about that person. You are entitled to tell your story, even if it feels treacherous.

When you write it, though, consider that the other person is a character in your book who deserves as much compassion as you do. Kim Barnes advises, "Treat nonfiction characters with the same complexity, compassion, etc., as [you would while writing] fiction. Know what their greatest fears and desires are. Otherwise you shouldn't be writing." In the following passage, Jillian Lauren further explains the attitude a memoirist ought to have toward her characters.

I always worry about the ethics of writing from life. I would only truly be concerned on the day I stopped worrying about it. I try to bring a compassionate attention to all of my characters while being aware that … when you reduce living, breathing people to two dimensions, something gets lost in translation. I tell people I've written about: "This character doesn't represent the totality of who you are; this character represents the role you played in this particular narrative."

It's also acceptable to write composite characters. In *Loose Girl*, I had so many friends during those years that it didn't make sense to include the ones that didn't matter to the story. There was also no reason to show that over the course of a few years, I had three different close friends who served the same purpose to the story. So I put various aspects of their personalities and appearances together, and I made up a name. Can one still call that a memoir, you might wonder? Yes, because memoir is not a journalistic recounting of facts; it's a story of memories.

You will also likely include some acquaintances or strangers in your memoir. These are the people we interact with briefly, who we will likely never see again. But they, too, deserve to be treated with a gentle pen. Gigi Little spoke about the complicated process of writing about strangers based on her experience of writing an essay titled "Sylvester," which was about her time working as a circus lighting director. The essay was about how she found a sense of belonging in the unlikeliest of places and how intimacy can develop between complete strangers.

This became the crux of my essay, finding intimacy in such a strange place—me on the coliseum floor, these guys way up in the rafters. At the time these stories were taking place, that moment had been special to me because of the trust in it. So special that I wanted to write about it. And to write about it was to break the trust.

Interestingly it didn't bother me to write about the other folks I profiled in the piece, dropping details about the worn-looking woman with dream-catcher earrings and the guy with seventies glasses and broken teeth. I didn't describe them as lovingly or delicately—

I just casually tossed their flaws on the page. But they
hadn't given me something.

How intimate should the details be? This, too, is a delicate subject
and should be treated on a case-by-case basis. When I wrote about
the stranger in the grocery store who suggested Ezra was autistic, I
did so with the purpose of clarifying that it's never helpful to the parents when strangers give advice. I disliked this woman immensely. She
stepped into a situation that was none of her business and effectively
ruined my day. Still, I had to find something human about her, something that made her a more rounded person than just the horrible thing
she unintentionally did to my family that day. So I described her hair
in a way that made clear she seemed harried, probably not her best
self. That small detail was useful in making her less of a monster, more
human, and just slightly worthy of compassion, even as she behaved
badly. Part of me wonders if I could have given her something else: a
pretty face, tasteful clothing, or a soft, kind voice. I could have made
clearer that she meant well. But one of the themes in *Seeing Ezra* is
my anger at how the world treated my family once it was clear Ezra
was developing differently from other children, and anger is something
few mothers are allowed in our culture without being considered mon-
sters themselves.

So that's how you may choose to deal with strangers. But what about
the friends and exes? How much detail should you include? The same
rules apply. Include what you must in order to serve the story, but don't
include details that are unnecessary. Stacy Pershall, author of *Loud
in the House of Myself: Memoir of a Strange Girl*, had to make a decision in the eleventh hour of her book's publication. She had included
a person in the memoir who had somehow gotten wind that Pershall
had written about her in the book. Without knowing anything about
how or why, this woman anonymously called the offices of Pershall's
publisher and threatened to sue them all. Pershall immediately determined who the woman was (because of the reported strong Southern

accent). The publishing staff met, and they determined that the best course of action would be for Pershall to make her character a man. So that's what she did.

Beginning memoir writers don't always understand that a writer can do this in memoir. It's not factual, but the truth of her character, the purpose the character served in the story, stayed the same, which is what's important. Consider how you, too, can change identifying details. Consider just how far you can take those changes without harming the character's purpose in the story. If it's important to the story that your old friend be overweight, by all means make her overweight. But then change something that doesn't matter: Make her blonde instead of brunette. Give her sharp green eyes. Anything that still feels true to distinguish her from her real-life self. And sometimes those changed facts feel *truer* than the reality. Maybe you see your friend as stunningly beautiful, even while much of the world doesn't.

TO CONTACT OR NOT TO CONTACT

Sometimes the person about whom you're writing still lives in town. Your friends know him. You are Facebook friends, or you know how to get in touch with her. It wouldn't take much to make contact, but should you? In general, the answer is: not before you write. Part of what defines memoir is the sacred process of being alone with your memories. Your story is yours alone. Yes, you have to write about your relationships with others, but the core of the story in memoir is about you—how you grew, what you learned, how you coped. Whatever inspires you to write is private, between you and your computer (or pen).

After you write the story, though, it might make sense to contact the people about whom you write. Hope Edelman found doing so to be useful before publishing her essay "The Sweetest Sex I Never

Had" in an anthology. The essay is about one of her first boyfriends and sexual experiences.

> I'm typically more concerned about writing about people from my past with whom I'm no longer in touch and don't know how to find. Even with the expansive reach of the Internet, some people from my distant past remain elusive. And for good reasons, [they] probably don't want to be found. ... I felt that as an adult thirty years later, he deserved his privacy and shouldn't be held accountable for anything he said or did when he was fifteen. Of course, everyone who knew me well back then knew who I was writing about, but that would have been only a very, very small percentage of readers, and they all knew he was a good egg, anyway. I did track him down after a lot of effort, to let him know the essay was coming out, and we wound up having a beautiful conversation by phone, reminiscing about that year. And I learned that one of my core beliefs about him from that time period—and a premise upon which the whole story had been based—hadn't been true at all, which could be a whole new essay unto itself one day.

By contacting the person, she reestablished a connection with him, something that may not have been possible otherwise. Additionally, the interaction provided her with fodder for more memoir writing.

WHAT TO EXPECT WHEN YOU WRITE ABOUT EXES, FRIENDS, AND OTHER PEOPLE YOU MIGHT PISS OFF

In *Loose Girl*, I wrote about a friend from high school who had treated me cruelly. She had also been kind. She had cared for me in many ways. But she needed to control our relationship at the time, and she did so by taking advantage of my lack of self-confidence and low self-esteem. I loved her. I also hated her. When I wrote the words about our friendship, I recounted the moments I most remembered, the ones that would best illuminate where I was emotionally at that time and why I kept making choices for myself that hurt me. After the book was published, she contacted me via e-mail. We had not spoken since I'd weaseled out of our friendship over twenty-five years earlier by dropping her for another friend. She said that she had a very different perception of herself back then and that she didn't appreciate being written about in that way. In truth, she sounded exactly as she had back in high school. Her angry e-mail only confirmed my view of her.

Others whom I'd written about also contacted me, happy to reconnect, pleased that I'd thought enough of them to write about them. Much like Hope Edelman, I had one phone call with a long-estranged friend, one I knew I'd hurt years back, and remembering everything, we cried, forgave one another, and, although we promised otherwise, never spoke again.

My ex-husband played a major role in my second memoir, *Seeing Ezra*, so I was very careful to protect his character, to show his immense goodness even as I showed the emotional distress between us that led to our marriage's end. I love my ex-husband very much. He's one of my closest friends. Our work as co-parents of our children remains sacred to me, and I refuse to do anything to destroy that, not even for my writing. But not everyone has this experience when marriages end. It's important to consider the reactions of people with whom you still have important relationships. I gave my ex-husband the book to read before it went to copyediting, but he refused. He said he trusted me and didn't want to have to re-experience the painful time we went through. But I think the offer was meaningful enough to him.

That said, before letting others read your finished product, decide what sort of leeway you are giving. If that person wants you to cut certain parts, or worse, pleads with you not to publish it at all, what will you do? Likewise, consider the myriad of responses that person may have. Be prepared. If you know that you won't change anything to make that person more comfortable, make that clear from the outset. In the following pages, you can read some other memoir writers' postpublication experiences. Judy Huddleston, author of *Love Him Madly*, a memoir about her love affair with The Doors singer Jim Morrison, didn't run into any problems. In fact, she got mostly positive reactions. However, she's aware of how social media has altered the potential effect on others.

> I didn't have any real changes in relationships. I believe it's okay to say something in memoir that I would be willing to say to someone's face (or at least write to them). However, I'd prefer to err on the side of caution. People come out of the woodwork when you think they're gone forever. For instance, I've got [an unpublished] high school memoir that I'd take certain scenes out of (or change names) since I now know the people again—largely due to Facebook. ... I was surprised that most reactions were positive; I'd worried that I was too "honest." By and large, people like to be written about.

Robert C. Rummel-Hudson wrote *Schuyler's Monster: A Father's Journey with His Wordless Daughter*, about what happened after his daughter was diagnosed with a neurological disorder. Within its pages, he recounts the affair he had during that difficult time. His daughter's reaction surprised him, especially since his in-laws felt differently.

> I tried to be honest and unbiased, but there were still a few ruffled feathers. [For the people] I was the most uncertain [about] (such as the woman with whom I had an affair—even though I changed her personal details and her name, she would still be identifiable to mutual

friends), I actually sent them parts of the book so they'd at least know what was coming.

Interestingly, my in-laws had problems with some minor details, enough so that I made changes in order to have the option of violence-free Thanksgivings in the future. But the former affair? [My mother-in-law] had no problem at all and even expressed her approval, both of the book in general and in her particular part in it.

EXERCISES

1. Write a scene in your memoir from the perspective of a person in your past whom you fear writing about, such as a former significant other or best friend. What happens to the scene when it is skewed toward someone else's reality?

2. Choose a former or current significant other or best friend featured prominently in your memoir. Write two short scenes consisting of your best and worst memories of this person. How do your portrayals of this person in the two scenes differ? How might these two exercises inform your portrayal of this person in your memoir?

3. Write a scene in your memoir that features one of your former best friends or significant others. Were there any unspoken fears you had or secrets you were keeping that affected that relationship? What secrets may they have been keeping? How may confessing those fears or secrets have affected the relationship then? What about now?

4. Imagine you're going to discuss a scene in your memoir with a former or current significant other or friend

featured in it. What might they take away from the scene? What are the key things you're trying to communicate in the scene? In what ways might your intended and received message be similar and different?

5. Write a scene in your memoir that takes place during your childhood or teenage years. Identify the emotions and reactions you had in the moment as your younger self. As an adult looking back on the moment, what are the things you wish you had known at the time about yourself and other people in the situation? How might your emotions and reactions have been affected by certain knowledge or wisdom you later gained?

6. Read a memoir about the author's relationship with friends, significant others, or other types of individuals featured in this chapter. How does the author deal with relationship power dynamics? Now think about these dynamics in your own relationships. How do they reveal themselves in your memoir? In what ways are they vital to understanding your relationships with others in your memoir?

WRITING THE REAL-TIME MEMOIR
Cris Mazza

As a result of writing my second memoir, *Something Wrong with Her*, I left my marriage, left my beloved house and gardened acreage, worked through a fraught reconciliation with a man I'd known when he was a boy, helped him come to terms with his choice to sacrifice his life for someone else's needs, and eventually helped him move 2,000 miles to start over again in the life he always felt he should have lived (with me).

But those weren't the reasons I started writing the book. In 2008, I found myself spending a lot of time on the floor with my dogs. Every novel I'd written had been published but hadn't led to the kind of satisfaction or fulfillment I'd instinctively been seeking. I was trying to say something, and it seemed no one could hear me. Not even myself. I'd researched a lot of material for my novels, from lighthouse legends to wildlife biologists to human trafficking, but the interior worlds of my characters and the baggage they stashed there orbited the same issues regarding sex.

An agent who'd become frustrated told me one of my manuscripts was "another middle-aged woman dealing with a self-imposed disability." I wondered: Why could I not feel "finished with" certain experiences and subjects? Why, after so many books, were certain things still so unresolved? Lying on the floor with my dogs was a way to avoid those kinds of questions, but I forced myself to get up and start another book, this time nonfiction, to tackle the material that kept reappearing in my novels.

I traveled back thirty years to try to understand how my sex life had gone so awry. The backwards expedition was, at first, only taken in my private studio, in the form of the manuscript for which the tangible research material included my previously published fiction, where my own secret bewilderment over what was wrong with me had been turned into the novels and stories about women with different careers, different goals, and different sensibilities, but all with peculiar responses to sex. Plus I had the thirty-year-old handwritten journals which had first captured some of who I was, Xeroxes of decades-old typewritten letters, and a variety of other paper artifacts kept by a person whose intuition suggested she might need them someday.

But in this case, the memoir journey was not confined to the baggage in my head (and stashes of paper I'd archived). The creating of the memoir turned into a real-time reconnection story. I ended up returning to a boy I'd left back there, to discover that he'd been waiting for me.

Just after starting to work on the manuscript—long before I realized what the book was supposed to be about—I prepared a small mailing for my personal extended mailing list to send a flier for a novel that was just released at that time. An envelope came to the top of the stack with his name. I thought, *Maybe Mark and I could be friends again,* and I included a business card with my contact info in his envelope.

Mark hadn't been "waiting" in the traditional sense. He'd lived without hope that he would ever see me again. He was not a modern-day Gatsby putting every breathing day of vigor into a plan that would undo the reasons we had not ended up together. In fact, almost every move he'd made had wrapped him further inside an existence of thankless obligation. He'd thought that "taking on" (his words) a woman without a high school diploma on the eve of divorce with no place to live with her two kids would give him a reason to persevere at the job that was supposed to be his calling, give him an accountability that would get him "through to the end of it."

Six months after sending my business card, still in the very early stages of writing the memoir I thought was only vaguely related to any past I'd shared with Mark, I received an e-mail from him. It couldn't have been more foretelling or appropriate: "Is this still your address? There are some things I want to tell you." I'd thought I was writing a memoir about a block of time I had purposely skipped in my first nonfiction book. I'd thought I was writing a memory-search for the reasons my sex life had been set on a path toward dysfunction or complete failure, based on my coming-of-age in the era when sexual-harassment laws were first germinating; when supervising teachers told their student-teachers to try masturbating; when prettier, more vivacious young women were considered more efficient employees; when fetching coffee for a male supervisor proved one's value to him. But I was actually on the verge of realizing I was writing a book about why I had not spent my life with Mark.

Once I realized my original intentions were going to lead no-where, once the real-time story of reconnecting with Mark began to affect both me and the book I was writing, I wanted to preserve the way the project was being modified by the actual journey backwards, how the manuscript morphed, how the morphing *is* the story the book wants to tell. I wanted to keep how both the reconnection story and the ongoing personal cogitation affected exactly *what* book was being written. I aimed for a book whose writing process needed to be read.

The crucial moment for both the book and the reconnection was when Mark asked me via e-mail what had gone wrong on an isolated night we were together in 1980—"two hours of my life that I was the happiest, most optimistic and secure," he said. It then became clear that a main aim for this book would be to answer him.

En route to finishing the book, while Mark and I struggled with decisions regarding our growing new (or old) relationship, more and more of that struggle became part of the book. Mark was present in the book in his e-mails to me and in comments he made while reading early drafts, which I included in the book as boxed sidebars or footnotes. The book went into production while we were still in transition but at least on a downhill slope toward resolution. Mark proofread, made more comments, elicited final revisions. By the time a shipment of galleys arrived, Mark had moved 2,000 miles east from California to begin the life with me that had been denied him the first time he asked in 1979.

Basically, while I wrote this book, something happened. Something happened while I was writing the book I *thought* I was going to write that turned it into another book altogether. Or it became the book—and then the life—it was supposed to be.

Cris Mazza's newest title is *Something Wrong with Her: A Real-Time Memoir* and chronicles the twenty-five-year journey to reunite with a boy from her past. She has sixteen other titles, including her most recent novel, *Various Men Who Knew Us as Girls*. Her first novel, *How to Leave a Country,* won the PEN/Nelson Algren Award for book-length fiction. Currently living fifty miles west of Chicago, she is a professor in the Program for Writers at the University of Illinois at Chicago.

THE TROUBLE WITH TELLING SOMEONE ELSE'S STORY
Lisa Dooley-Rufle

We all know the adage that says what we put out into the universe comes back to us, but no matter how accustomed we get to this concept of a divine balancing of the scales, it never makes being on the receiving end easy. Especially when it involves writing about a loved one's poor personal choices. Because once you set those words loose into the world, you no longer control the impact they will have when they hit their target.

It all started with the need for me to deal with my husband's DWI arrest. I had no way of processing what was happening, so

I just wrote it all out. There was no contemplation or carefully constructed pros/cons list involved; I simply resorted to my usual coping mechanism of putting words on paper. The essay itself metamorphosed many times. It started off as being an angry piece meant to punish my husband for his bad decision. In the end, after some heavy editing, it turned into a tangible piece of written therapy. Through this simple act, I gained the perspective and distance needed to get over this particular hurdle in my marriage. Or so I thought.

I thought nothing more of this essay for some time. It had served its cathartic and therapeutic purpose and was saved as some anonymous Word file on my laptop—until I had the brilliant idea of making this utterly personal and private story public by pitching it to the website *xoJane* as an It Happened to Me piece. Clearly something transpired inside my head that convinced me that sharing this essay was a good idea, though I have no recollection of what that something actually was. Maybe it was the fact that this was someone else's story and not my own that made the decision seem effortless. Despite the fact that I keep my demons heavily guarded under lock and key, I treated other people's with far less care. Maybe somewhere deep down I knew that telling my story through the filter of my husband's experience would help me get over it once and for all.

To my surprise, my essay was accepted for publication. I was elated. It didn't cross my mind that publishing my piece would have any negative ramifications. In my head the piece would be read only by those who regularly visited the *xoJane* website. And clearly since my husband was not their target demographic, he would be none the wiser. But I must've had an inkling of a conscience about my choice in writing subjects because I was careful about who saw it when I shared it on social media. I regularly interacted with family members through Facebook, and I didn't want to disclose my husband's struggle to them, so I was especially careful to adjust the privacy settings of any posts I made pertaining to the essay.

But while I was carefully covering my own tracks, I forgot another important life law: the one that says we have zero control over anyone else's actions. So, of course, through the wonders of Facebook, a well-meaning friend posted on my wall something along the lines of not knowing about my husband's incident and preaching a bunch of recovery dogma. For those of you who are unfamiliar with the technicalities of Facebooking, this was a faux pas because had this friend commented directly on my posting of the article, her comments would not have been visible to the people I was trying to keep this hidden from. But because she posted something independent of my top-secret-but-not-really post, everyone who was my friend could see her comments. This is where the trouble began.

While I was able to run interference and block her post from my general friend population (aka hubby's family), the damage had already been done. In an attempt to save face and my relationship, I came clean to my husband. I told him how I wrote an essay about how his DWI and subsequent arrest affected me. I told him that it had been published on a somewhat well-trafficked website and that I published it under my actual name so there was a chance that someone in real life would know who he was and what he had gone through. Yet another important life lesson: Once it's on the Internet, it can't be undone.

As expected, this caused some tension in our relationship. The balance of trust was totally knocked off kilter. I went into this being the better person (in my head at least). I was the one who had been wronged. I came out the other side as someone who had, in the most simplified way, tried to capitalize on my husband's mistake for the sake of my art. I had to own up to the fact that while it may be the norm as a personal essay writer to share private stories or to overshare, it is not okay to tell someone else's story without his or her permission. I fought this idea for a long time. I tried to justify it to myself by claiming that I had written it from *my* point of view. And while that was indeed true, I should have taken some steps to ensure that it was okay to share my story against the backdrop of someone else's.

After this incident, I was afraid to write. I became accustomed to second-guessing every time I made mention of someone or something in a piece of writing. Events became something that needed to be reconstructed with precision; otherwise they could be misinterpreted as lies. Dialogue needed to be verbatim; otherwise how could I truthfully re-create the moment? Even when I made a passing mention of someone who played a bit part in the story I was sharing, I felt the need to ask him for his permission. And this, as any writer of memoir can attest, is not always possible or desired.

While things in my marriage could have turned out much worse as a result of my choosing to use my husband as subject material, I feel as if I learned many important lessons about writing as well as life. While my essay had a direct, visible, and short-lived effect on my husband, it had more of an indirect but long-lasting effect on me. My writing suffered because I found it difficult to trust myself in the writing process and in my ability to tell my story without bringing to the forefront the stories of other people. I wasn't sure where their story ended and mine began.

Even though time has passed, I still hesitate to share my writing. I have been keeping my work hidden away like a dirty secret for fear of misrepresenting others and having it come back to haunt me. I guess that is the price we pay as personal essay writers. We have this desire to share such intimate parts of ourselves that we lack the capacity to censor when appropriate. We don't have the luxury of camouflaging our stories, because to do so would cheapen the integrity of the work. While fiction writers can disguise this in their characters and poets can paint the truth around elaborate word schemes, we put it all out there, for better or worse. When we choose to write about our personal experiences, we don't get any say in how it is interpreted once we give it wings. We cannot hide behind any illusions that what we wrote is anything less than the complete truth. We make our proverbial bed, and we have to lie in it. That's a heavy dose of reality.

Lisa Dooley-Rufle is a freelance writer living on Long Island, New York. She is the mom of a preschooler and two fur kids of the feline persuasion. Being surrounded by males in the home, she tends to keep the girl power cranked up to 11 at all times. She will beg, borrow, and steal for a little "me time," which she likes to fill by reading anything she can get her hands on, dabbling in photography, and laughing too loudly at countless Internet cat videos. You can visit her at lisarufle.blogspot.com.

WHEN YOU CAN'T HURT HIM ANYMORE
Rachel Ament

It is easier to write about people, which incidentally means hurting people, when you don't know them anymore. You know they are out there, somewhere, like the sun or the future. But they are still just amorphous ideas. You don't worry about hurting ideas. Or stay up all night considering the thousands of ways ideas can misinterpret your writing.

When I was twenty-four, I wrote an essay for an obscure online Jewish magazine. Like so much of my writing at the time, the essay was about a date gone wrong with a guy I had met at a Jewish event. This someone (we'll call him Jerry) had a certain hunger about him, a very New York-style hunger. He seemed to be hungry for power and status, but what he was really after was acceptance.

There is a bit of Jerry's hunger in us all, but he never thought to hide any of it or even to be subtle about it. Jerry threw all his wants and ambitions at me at once. Within minutes of meeting me, he told me about how he worked in ad sales, about how he was "freakin'" successful, about how he had a sweet-ass apartment, about how he had everything he had ever wanted or needed except for that one thing: a girlfriend. If he could just have a girlfriend, someone to hold and cradle him when he came home at night, then everything else would fit into place.

My essay focused on and jeered at Jerry's hunger. I, of course, knew there was more to him than that; there is more to everyone than just their surface traits and needs. But at the time, I didn't see the problem with writing about only a part of a person, the part I could see the most and that would entertain and amuse the most. I thought I was writing honestly. I was writing what I saw. But I didn't realize that writing should be about more than seeing; it should also be about feeling and searching.

When you are writing, it's so tempting to skim surfaces. We just want to tell the parts that we think the reader wants to hear. I didn't know Jerry anymore and knew he would never track down the essay, so couldn't I just skip to the funny parts? The outrageous parts? Wasn't it okay to make Jerry look like an idiot? At this point, Jerry was some sketchy smudge in my mind. And a smudge seemed like something that could be insulted!

And insult I did. Jerry and I talked at great length, and most of it was pretty unmemorable. So you're from Kentucky? What was that like? Lots of horses? I bet you like horses! But other moments were more absurd. Jerry was a pretty harmless guy, but he had that kind of cheesy charisma that only comes out in someone when they are trying to impress others. This kind of giddy desperation generally comes from a place of hurt and sadness. But it can also be pretty funny. Extreme personalities can be funny. When someone is too much, when they cross every limit, when they don't know when to stop, you can't help but laugh.

Writing about Jerry never felt good, even at the time. I kept telling myself it was okay, that Jerry would never see the story or be hurt by it. We existed in different corners of the Internet. And if he would never be hurt, then who would be? But without sounding like someone who makes all her clothes out of woven hemp and grapeseed-scented incense, I think a lot about what energies I'm putting out into the world. Even if feelings aren't directly being hurt, I know that throwing negative sentiments and feelings out there can wreck and destroy. Every time we speak ill of someone, even through writing, that harshness moves through the air. The world moves with and towards the harshness and then eventually absorbs it.

But I was only twenty-four and still at that negligent stage of writing when I thought being a writer meant truth over feelings, that it meant an unsettled conscience. I believed the world needed to be recorded, and sometimes those records came at other people's expense. The world needed to laugh. And what would we laugh about if not people? A tree? A flower?

Jerry was easy to laugh at. Our first (and only) date practically hemorrhaged with "material." We were seeing a movie in Brooklyn, and Jerry was being even more forward and aggressive than he had been the night we met. He seemed ready for some kind of plunge. Not marriage, exactly, but something close to it. He seemed to want the idea of matrimony to be near us, close enough for us to catch a whiff of it and take in its clean, flowery scent.

On our way to the movie, Jerry was petting my hand and telling me how much he wanted to be with me. I nodded distractedly, staring out the window, trying to keep up with the view. I was thinking about other boys, boys who had hurt me and had torn at me. That is what being trapped in a car with a guy you can't stand will do to you. It will make you miss every other guy who is not him.

Jerry honked his car horn noisily. He was pulling up to a house, a boring, perfect house, like the kind I grew up in. I jostled abruptly awake. I suddenly realized where we were: at Jerry's parents' house. Jerry explained that he wanted to introduce me to his mom. Yes, that's right. He wanted to introduce me to his mom on the first date. To be fair, this wasn't *that* big of an event. I never did meet his mom, just saw a dim shape of her, standing maternally on the front porch. I refused to get out of the car. I simply couldn't go through with it. I told Jerry I had a headache, that it was *serious*, that I needed to be taken home that instant.

But I am, of course, a *writer*, or at least was trying to be. When writing the account of that first date, I didn't lie, pad, or embellish. I didn't add any dramatic flourishes that weren't there. But what I did do was tell the story in this awful, brassy, bratty tone, the kind that seems like it is laughing at not just people in the story but at the entire world.

Laughter is usually something you give people as a gift. You are telling people they are funny. They are loved. Ha ha ha ha ha. A ha ha ha ha ha ha. But when you are laughing *at* people, those same easy, hearty sounds turn sharp. You are pounding at them, letting them know: *There is something wrong with you. There is something wrong with you. There is something wrong with you.*

There should be some kind of writer's rule that you shouldn't be able to write about someone unless you still know them. Or you know they are going to read it. Writers need checks and balances. We shouldn't have the power and range to do whatever we want with a character simply because we don't think they are watching. Our writing starts to only hit on the loudest moments, the most disruptive moments. And then all the characters fall flat.

Last summer, I wrote an introduction for an anthology I was compiling and editing called *The Jewish Daughter Diaries: True Stories of Being Loved Too Much By Our Moms.* I made fun of my mom in the story, poked and prodded at her overprotectiveness, her neuroticism. But all of my jabs were shrouded in love and care. I was protecting her. Because ... she is my *mom.* I knew my mom would read it and would probably even get her hands on a draft before the book was published. And as I wrote, I could hear her in my head, judging but also being judged. *Oh, that is funny. Oh, you are such a hoot. Wait, I don't think you should include that part. Please, Rachel, you're not as funny as you think you are.*

Some say that being too aware of your subject makes writing turn soft. But softness isn't necessarily a weakness. When you are thinking about how your subject will respond, it forces you to question your own writing, to see the full shape of things. You can't just lay on attacks. You have to write the other side of it. You have to make the writing complete.

Creating complete pictures makes writing more intimate. You feel like you know the characters. And when it comes time for the more absurd moments, the readers will feel like they are laughing at the misadventures of an awkward but endearing friend. When we layer our characters with inconsistencies and complexities, the reader becomes more invested and the story becomes funnier. We crave depth even when all we are trying to do is laugh.

I owe it to my subjects to care about them, even when I don't think they're watching. It's the least I can do. That person has given me something worth writing about: a memory, a funny moment, a change in perspective. They deserve to be written about with attention and care.

After I wrote the introduction for the anthology, I had to write my own essay for the collection. There was a word count I was trying desperately to meet. The collection was due in a few weeks, and I felt empty inside with writer's block. I was all dead space. No inspiration, nothing. I thought about that over-the-top essay I'd written about Jerry. Even though I wrote it when I was only twenty-four and it would need some fine-tuning, I thought it would be perfect for the collection. The essay discussed my Jewish mom, how she pushed me to go on that date with Jerry, to give guys like Jerry a chance. The essay really nailed what the anthology was about: moms who worry too much because they love too much.

Months later, when the manuscript was e-mailed to the publisher and probably already at the printing press, I felt that shaky feeling in my gut. I had done it again. This essay about Jerry, this essay that was true but didn't feel true and was probably missing some truths, would be out there again but even more so. I knew Jerry still wouldn't read it. The essay was marketed to females. It had a preteen title and a sappy Chicken Soup for the Soul-style cover. We had been on only one date, and I never even gave him my last name, so it wasn't like he had been spending the past eight years Googling me. Besides, even if he did read it, it all happened so long ago that he probably wouldn't even be hurt by it. I didn't use his real name.

But it didn't matter. There was that harshness again. That harshness that moved through the air and took us all with it. I wondered if I would ever learn how to let the harshness move without me, to watch it slide right past me and not feel its pull.

Rachel Ament is a writer, editor, and complainer living in Washington, D.C. She has been published in *The New York Times*, *The Jerusalem Post*, *Oxygen*, *AOL*, *HelloGiggles*, and other publications. She was the head writer for the New Orleans-based film *Nola* and edited *The Jewish Daughter Diaries: True Stories of Being Loved Too Much By Our Moms*, a collection of essays exploring the complex, colorful, and, at times, claustrophobic relationship between Jewish mothers and daughters.

WHY I TURNED DOWN
THE NEW YORK TIMES
Sage Cohen

Words have always been my magic carpet ride through experience to understanding. In the early days of my divorce, when I was a barn burning down, I wrote words of destruction, rage, revenge. When the smoke cleared and I could see the moon, I wrote grief—and followed it all the way back to my childhood. Story by story, I picked the bones of my past clean. I fully digested my choices, my disappointments, my hopes, and my hurts until I came to a wide-open field of acceptance. Grace.

In time, I wanted to send stories from this rooted and sure place in me up to the surface where other divorcing parents were just starting to go under. I wanted to offer them a lifeline. I registered the name radicaldivorce.com, and I set out to create a blog that would serve as a virtual kitchen table where I could sit down with a box of tissues and a cup of tea, and welcome parents struggling to find their way forward into new incarnations of self and family.

I hired a lovely woman to help me architect and design the blog. As we set out to strategically deliver on my vision, I culled from a few years' worth of writing fifty or so short essay posts and fifty poems to get me started. I was fanatically focused on delivering extraordinary content to my most cherished imaginary audience. So focused that I had neglected to consider one rather significant reader: my ex-husband, Pete.

* * * * *

The night before the blog's go-live date, I woke in a sweat. I was about to go public with some of the most intimate stories of my marriage, some of the most explosive pain of my life. And Pete was the antagonist in the crosshairs of my investigation. As the father of my five-year-old son, Pete would be a person of primary importance in my life for many years to come. I had no blueprint for navigating my responsibility to my truth in tandem with my responsibility to my family.

Now, Pete married a writer. And he divorced a writer. And the liabilities of such choices are obvious. He knew loosely of my Radical Divorce aspirations: that my goal was to help people cultivate the kind of child-centered, collaborative friendship that we had worked so hard to establish. But he was not aware of the years of personal process I had gone through to get there. He had been spared the excruciating details of my quest to forgive him, forgive myself, make my peace, and rebuild my happiness from the ground up. These were the stories I intended to tell.

While I didn't feel that I needed Pete's permission, I felt I owed him a heads-up. At the end of that anguished night, I delayed the blog's launch date and arranged a meeting. This became a galvanizing moment in my writing career.

I created a manifesto of sorts where I articulated for myself, in writing, some bylaws of personal essay and memoir writing. Here I clarified my moral position on the healing power of truth telling—no matter how ugly the facts might be. I fortified my courage for the inevitable backlash that comes with taking an unpopular public position. And I anchored my own integrity in what I intended to share and how. Then I was ready to include Pete.

* * * * *

Looking out through the Plexiglas dividing our son's indoor soccer class from our little wobbly table, I explained to him that yes, Radical Divorce would celebrate our happily-ever-after blended family where Pete and his post- and pre-wives routinely attend birthday parties together and confuse all the grandparents. But more important, it would meet parents in their most frightened and wobbly places, and invite them to explore the opportunities to make a bad situation better for their kids—and for themselves.

Yes, Pete deserved a great deal of credit for meeting me halfway, but I could not tell his story. I could only tell my own and show how the choices I made helped us arrive at a deeper trust and kindness in divorce than we ever approached in marriage. If I was going to help anyone, I explained, I was going to need to expose my most broken and hollowed-out places in order to trace an authentic trajectory to our family's current relative peace and ease.

First Pete was scared. Then defensive. "If you're the hero of your story, that makes me the villain," he countered.

"Yes, once I saw you as a villain, and that is part of the story. But then I made a choice to see you as a teacher. And this is my position. We came together and apart in ways that I needed, to go deeper in my evolution as a person. And the deeper I go, the more capable I am as Teddy's mother and your co-parent. I will share ugly moments that hurt me—not to make you wrong but to explore how we worked together to make it right. You can trust that I mean you no harm."

His shoulders went down, and his voice softened. The wild eyes of our rocky years gave way to a more sure and steady vision. Pete told me he trusted me to tell our story responsibly. I thanked him for his trust. The blog went live.

* * * * *

The tricky thing about telling the truth is that there is no single truth. A diamond causes endless refractions, and so do the events we live through. How we dig a moment up, shape it, and polish it influences what we can see and feel at any given time. But this process is in constant flow, as we are. For me, the distance between what happened and what was experienced is best bridged in story. Through writing, I instruct myself about how to integrate who I've been with who I'm becoming.

* * * * *

A few months into Radical Divorce, a Facebook friend and reader of my blog introduced me to a *New York Times* columnist who was writing about divorce. I spoke to the journalist for an hour as part of a pre-interview for her column that ran a reportage-style he said/she said look at why couples divorce. I thought it would be an interesting opportunity for Pete to have a voice in our story and for us to explore how our stories (each procured through independent interviews) aligned—or didn't.

As the journalist pressed me for my thesis statement about why our marriage ended, I became increasingly uncomfortable. I was giving her metaphors about the mismatch of my depths and Pete's heights, but she wanted facts.

"Remember that New Yorkers are going to be reading this article. They're going to want to understand what actually happened here," she advised, steering me toward the clincher.

The problem wasn't that I had grown too "woo-woo" since moving to the West Coast to give a clear, factual answer. Though it took me a few hours after our call to understand, the problem was that I was fundamentally opposed to giving such an answer.

Pete and I had not betrayed each other in any kind of conventional way. There had been no affair. No lies or deceit or violence. I had a very specific moment to point to when I knew that it was over, but this was my moment and it was hinged to a lifetime of moments that could not be summed up in one sentence. There seemed no way to say it without blame. And this was the whole point of my project—to move away from blame and instead seek the opportunities of each heartbreak and hardship.

I knew enough from a lifetime of storytelling to expect that twenty years from now, Pete and I would likely each have a sentence or two that distilled the entire experience of our relationship to a "why it ended" synopsis. Maybe we'd even use the same two sentences. But it was all still too fresh. I was still writing myself out of the hole. I could not send the arrow of a summary statement through my heart or his. Whatever I might say would not be true enough and might not even be true at all.

What I discovered after speaking to this journalist is that I was not willing to let anyone, not even *The New York Times*, have a say in how I tell my story or decide which were the pertinent moments to lift up out of the whole blurry mess of years.

Mining, shaping, and polishing the story was all I had. I needed to find my way with it. I'd deliver the "how I knew it was over" thesis statement when I was good and ready. When I felt I could do so responsibly. In a way that my son could digest when he came upon it someday. In a way that my ex-husband's extended family could breathe in. In a way that I could live with, knowing that nothing we say is true for much longer than the moment when it passes through our lips or our storytelling fingers.

* * * * *

I was terrified that speaking my truth would destroy our tenuously reconstructed family, but the opposite proved to be true. Radical Divorce has brought Pete and me closer. The more I write, the more compassion I have for both of us. And the more I scrape blame clean out of the clay, the more supple and collaborative our co-construction becomes.

Writing has taught me to live with the imprecision of truth. To tend it with my words and my devotion. And to let the stories carve new passages through me as they flow back to their source, without holding on too tight to them.

I don't know if Pete has ever read the blog. I don't know if he ever will. But I write with love for his humanity and for mine. With love for our mistakes, our anguish, our broken little mending family. All of us have been stretched in new directions. Just as they say smiling can make you happy, writing has a similar capacity to shape emotion. Committing to a fierce respect of my co-parent on the page called me back to a respect for him in everyday life that I had lost along the way. Honoring him as the father of my child and the dark angel of some of my most complicated life lessons has helped me honor the wisdom that grief and rage bring.

Staying with the story, as it turns out, is very much like staying with the co-parent. The marriage ends, but the family continues. Word by word, we find our way.

Sage Cohen is the author of *Writing the Life Poetic: An Invitation to Read and Write Poetry* and *The Productive Writer: Tips & Tools to Help You Write More, Stress Less & Create Success*, both from Writer's Digest Books, and the poetry collection *Like the Heart, the World* from Queen of Wands Press. Her poems, essays, short stories, and how-to articles appear in publications including *Rattle*; *Poetry Flash*; *Hip Mama* magazine; *The Night, and the Rain, and the River*; *A Cup of Comfort for Writers: Inspirational Stories that Celebrate the Literary Life*; *Writer's Digest* magazine; *Poet's Market*; and *Writer's Market*. She offers strategies and support for writers at pathofpossibility.com and for divorcing parents at radicaldivorce.com.

CHAPTER FIVE

shame me twice

WRITING ABOUT SEX, DRUGS, AND BAD BEHAVIOR

"It is more about what can be gleaned from a section of one's life than about the outcome of the life as a whole."

—GORE VIDAL, *PALIMPSEST: A MEMOIR*

The other day, my son told me a story about how his friend got hurt while playing kickball because some kid threw the ball way too hard. His friend had to go to the nurse's office and sit with a pack of ice on his cheek for the rest of the period. The next day, he came to me crying. "I'm the one who threw the ball that hurt him," he confessed.

Owning our bad behavior is one of the hardest things memoir writers have to do. Since the time we were young, we feel terrible shame about our mistakes. My son is no exception. If he grows up to write a memoir, this struggle will be important for him. I don't wish him this struggle, yet I wouldn't want to deny him of it either. One of the great joys of memoir writing is battling myself on the page, getting the younger me pinned down to confess her ugly truths. By doing that, by challenging myself in this way to say, *Yes, I did that*, I know that I'm freeing both my readers and myself from our shame. Abby Mims says, "What are you really sharing or helping the reader with if you don't show most or all of [your] dark, ugly places? Not much."

Let's face it: We all do horrible things from time to time. The difference between a memoirist and someone who isn't a memoirist is that a memoir writer does horrible things in public for everyone to see. Or, more accurately, a memoir writer *confesses* to those horrible things on the page. When you've been abused or hurt in some real way, you will be hard-pressed to find someone who will condemn you for what happened to you. But when *you* are the agent of the bad behavior, i.e., sexual deviance, addiction, gambling, and so on, you take on the burden of having to admit that. Those who don't know what it's like to make bad choices at huge cost to your life or others' can't understand why you would ever do the things you did, so it's your job as a memoirist to make those reasons clear.

SHOULD YOU TELL THIS STORY?

Just because you lived a life of crime, lost your license because of DUIs, or had sex with three hundred people before the age of thirty doesn't necessarily mean you have a memoir. What you have is an interesting story, probably a shocking one at times. But a memoir is not just a shocking story. It's a story of how those shocking events matter to you. It's how you make sense of that story. Ultimately it's how that understanding of your story shows your readers something they need to know about themselves, about human beings in general, or about the world.

Supposing you do have a memoir to write, here are some considerations.

- Are you ready to expose yourself in this way? How will such a confession affect your life, your career, your family, etc.?
- Are you ready to be as vulnerable on the page as you will need to be? In order to write well about bad behavior, you have to get to the core of your emotional experience at the time.
- Secrets may be revealed. Perhaps you stole from your grandparents to pay for drugs. Perhaps you had sex with your best friend's husband. What will be the result of these sorts of confessions for you and the other people involved at the time?

HOW TO WRITE ABOUT SEX, DRUGS, AND BAD BEHAVIOR

WRITE ARTFULLY

To write this memoir, you have to be willing to descend to some pretty dark places. Most of our bad behavior is simply a mask for much darker, harder feelings, such as despair, emptiness, and desperation. In her essay for *The New York Times*, "Make Me Worry You're Not O.K.," Susan Shapiro wrote about seeing this sort of depth in some of her students' work.

> You can't remain removed and dignified and ace it. I do promise my students, though, that through the art of writing, they can transform their worst experience into the most beautiful. I found that those who cried while reading their piece aloud often later saw it in print. I believe that's because they were coming from the right place—not the hip, but the heart.[1]

Memoir allows you to find redemption in some of the worst things that have happened in your life and some of the worst things you've done,

---

1 opinionator.blogs.nytimes.com/2012/12/31/make-me-worry-youre-not-o-k

by bringing out the authenticity of your experience. Memoir allows you to mold your messy experiences into an artful shape.

Here's something else to know about memoir—or maybe it's something to know about addiction, sadness, or being human: Sadness is also longing, and longing is beautiful in words. When you write about that time that you sunk the needle into your arm, or the time you kissed the woman from forehead to toes, just so you could get back to that feeling of being desired, or the time you poured yourself the first scotch after having been on the wagon for five years, watching the amber liquid hit the ice, practically feeling it in your throat, you are really writing about yearning to feel those chemicals again. I call it addiction porn. You have resolved to not ruin your life anymore, but man, remember how good it felt to think you were going to be free of your pain? Remember that promise of freedom? It was an absolute lie. But believing in it was real.

WRITE WITH REFLECTION

With that in mind, the difference between you then and you now is that you *don't* believe in it anymore. You might miss believing in it, but that's because you don't. On his blog, William Pryor (author of *The Survival of the Coolest*) warns against getting too lost in that old feeling.

> My name is on the cover, my family and friends in the story—I had to do justice to this exposure by avoiding blame games and petty larceny of their feelings. And yet the transparent telling of such a narrative, avoiding "war stories" and boasting of depths of degradation—when I get it right—touches and inspires the reader's experience of being human, as many have told me. It is in the depths, the extremes, that we can see our humanity.[2]

Don't make a spectacle of your bad behavior. Be reflective. Provide perspective. Otherwise you're just bragging about being a jerk. When

---

2 williampryor.wordpress.com

you write memoir, you need to give your readers some understanding, some wisdom to hold onto. Caroline Knapp's *Drinking: A Love Story* is rich with passages like this one below.

> Liquor creates delusion. It can make your life feel full of risk and adventure, sparkling and dynamic as a rough sea under sunlight. A single drink can make you feel unstoppable, masterful, capable of solving problems that overwhelmed you just five minutes before. In fact, the opposite is true: Drinking brings your life to a standstill, makes it static as rock over time.[3]

She doesn't just tell the way drinking became central in her life; she constantly gives us insight as to why, clarifying what the drinking did for her. As a result, the reader comes away with a new understanding of how drinking felt necessary to her. We care for her. We learn from her.

WRITE HONESTLY

Memoir is, by definition, an exercise in honesty. But when you write about your poor behavior, there is an added difficulty to being honest. That's partly because it can feel terrible to take full responsibility. Usually, if we go astray, it's because initially we were victims of something, e.g., abuse, bad influences, or abandonment. How hard it is to move past that simple truism and find what else is there. Not everyone behaves badly. What was inside us that made us make these choices? Because we *did* make those choices; nobody held guns to our heads. William Pryor's discussion of myth is deeply important regarding memoir.

> I did whatever I could to find out what happened from surviving friends, family, and media, but that is simply a skeleton upon which the story is draped. This is the unmasking of the myth, and, as Jean Cocteau put it: "Man seeks to escape himself in myth and does so by

---

[3] Caroline Knapp, *Drinking: A Love Story* (New York: Delta Books, 1996), p.166.

any means at his disposal. Drugs, alcohol, or lies. Unable to withdraw into himself, he disguises himself. Lies and inaccuracy give him a few moments of comfort." I wanted to go beyond a re-creation of the past to discover meaning in the degradation of my addiction experience. The past is another country and not my prime interest. It's more what the past can tell us about how we deal with the present moment.

How easy it might be to glorify the self by recounting one's past. How pretty and packaged it might seem to look back on that awful time and picture oneself as purely a victim of one's circumstances or, alternatively, as only a selfish drug addict. This issue of "unmasking myths," as Pryor calls it, is true of all memoir, but it is perhaps most notable in memoirs about deviant behavior. Your job in memoir is to write *your* story, which means quieting the sometimes loud narratives that are handed to us by the larger culture.

Allow me to explain further. When I was trying to write *Loose Girl*, about my complicated relationship with boys and men, it took me many years of writing and rewriting to get to the truth about my story. Here is an essay I wrote for *Brevity*, a nonfiction literary journal, about that process.

> *Loose Girl: A Memoir of Promiscuity* took five months to write, but I spent almost ten years figuring out what this book was really about. To be honest, I spent almost ten years working on a single scene—the first full scene in the book. I rewrote that scene again and again, each time knowing I had not gotten it right. I knew there was something about this scene, something more meaningful than what I was getting at, something more profound. I tried writing it as an essay. I tried workshopping it in groups. I was told, "Keep writing." So I did.

I pulled up that same file on my computer and delved inside it yet again, trying to find what there was to find, knowing I had not gotten to its bottom yet.

The scene is from when I was twelve years old and living in New Jersey. Two friends and I ventured into Manhattan by ourselves one night to meet up with boys we didn't know, and we wound up leaving in the early morning hours because one of my friends had an argument with one of the boys. We took the subway up to the Port Authority near the George Washington Bridge and then took a bus from there to get back home. Because of the hour, though, the bus only went to a town about ten miles from my home, so we were stuck.

We found an all-night gas station where two attendants promised to drive us home at the end of their shift. They did, and in the car, one of those men slid his hand up my leg and grabbed my crotch. I knew from the first time I wrote this scene that it was about danger, about three girls going into the city at night seeking danger of some sort and, in the end, finding it. For a long time, I thought of myself in this scene as a victim because that man molested me. This was certainly a part of the truth, but it wasn't the whole truth. I rewrote the scene and the moment when he molested me at least fifteen times. And then, one day, I was able to write a truth about that moment that I had been too ashamed, too frightened, to admit before:

> I squirm, but it's no use. His coarse fingers worm up to my underwear, scratching and grabbing as I try to pull away. They're my best underwear, lavender in color, and he traces the edges with his fingertips. I put them on that evening with

the thought that just maybe I would get to third base with one of the boys from the city. It seems a long time ago that we were in my house, full of expectation, getting ready for the night. Now he holds his fingers against my crotch—not inside, just against—letting me know he is there. I clench my body, my eyes turned to the window. I want to scream, to push his hand away, but I'm too afraid. Too afraid if I don't give in, he won't let me go at all. But there's something else, too, something growing inside me, something I don't really want to admit: There's another part that's not afraid at all. I almost like it. I know what's happening isn't right. But his touch is an inevitable result of the evening. It is my greatest hope—to be wanted. And here, with this repulsive older man, I am getting that. He holds his hand there like he owns me, but really, silently, I'm the one who owns him.

The day I wrote this version of that moment, the *truest* version of that moment, is the day I started writing *Loose Girl*. This theme in my life, this terrible, shameful theme—that I would take attention from men any way I could because it made me feel in control and loved—is the theme that would drive my memoir forward. I wrote the rest of the book swiftly, with no difficulty. The words poured forth like water.

Many times, when writers attempt to write their stories, they aren't willing to look closely. Too much pain, shame, or fear stands like a guard at the door. But if you can relax into those feelings, if you can sit with your flawed, imperfect self, silence your internal judge, and allow yourself to write toward meaning, you just might locate the truth that holds the key to your entire book. [4]

How graphic should you get? How much should you reveal about the details of your sex addiction, your messy affair, or your methamphetamine use? The answer is: *all of it.* Let us see the human, horrible nitty-gritty of how you smoked meth in the stained gas station bathroom while your three-year-old waited in the car. Life is messy. It is ugly and raw and sexy and beautiful. It is all of those things. If you leave out the details, the small things that bring your readers that much more into the experience, then you aren't honoring that complexity. Life makes us all uncomfortable. Inside that discomfort, we blossom new parts of ourselves. Give that gift to your readers, too.

WRITE THE TRUE ENDING

After I got about one hundred pages into *Loose Girl*, I didn't know where to go next. I shared the pages with a writing colleague, and she told me that while I'd explicated the story of my problem, now readers would want to know how I got to where I was after the fact: a counselor, a writer, and married with two children. So I set out to reveal the *very slow* transition from who I was then to who I came to be. And here's the truth about those two different people: *They were the same person.* I wasn't actually all that different. I just made different choices; I wasn't behaving the same way. But the pull of men was still inside me.

Still, like one of my editors once told me, "America loves a redemption story." And the truth was also that I *had* reached some level of recovery, albeit a small one. Without that bit of a story, like my writer friend had intimated, there wouldn't be a complete arc.

Many times, memoir students ask me about ending their memoirs. How do they end the story when, of course, the story lives on because they're still alive? The answer is that the end of the memoir is simply the end of that particular arc in your life. If your story is about

---

4 www.creativenonfiction.org/brevity/craft/craft_cohen1_10.htm

being a Ritalin addict, then the story ends when you finally got clean for good. The ending includes your ongoing struggle against the addiction. Maybe you write about how that desire still sometimes creeps up and, while you can't know for sure that you'll never use again, you know that you aren't going to do it today. That's an ending. If your story is about how you've been a kleptomaniac your whole life and you have decided that you must never steal again because you have children now, that's an ending. There is no way you've found full resolve. Life isn't like that. Life is messy, unruly, and unpredictable. Your job in memoir is to make sense of it, to show that you are by no means perfect, not then and not now, and to show us the ending—the *truth*—that *best* ties up your story arc.

WHAT TO EXPECT WHEN YOU WRITE ABOUT SEX, DRUGS, AND BAD BEHAVIOR

Memoirists get raked over the coals. We are called selfish, narcissistic, egotistical, and awash in our own self-importance. Now consider the kinds of things that a number of us confess to doing: taking drugs, wrecking cars, leaving people behind, and hurting others. I once said in an interview that writing a memoir as a woman is dangerous enough, but writing a memoir as a woman and talking about my sex life? I may as well give other people the darts. In this age of blogging, trolling, and the notion that absolutely anyone is entitled to have an opinion, you will need to prepare yourself for the attack, because it will come. Strangers and people who know you will misconceive your experience. They will decide you are a terrible person. They will decide they hate you, never having met you, because you are showing them parts of themselves they may not want to see.

However, if you tell your truth honestly and vulnerably, you will also get messages from people—complete strangers—who are moved by your story, who see themselves in your words. You will prevent some people from killing themselves or from further abusing drugs. You will give people hope that they can get better, like you did. Hopefully, their voices will seem louder to you than those of your detractors.

Be aware that you do need to be more careful when sharing information about other people in your book using drugs or prostituting or otherwise doing things that are illegal in most states. People who you write about are more likely to take legal action if you write about them doing things that can get them in trouble with the law or family members. Chapter seven provides a full discussion of the legalities of memoirs.

Similarly, consider your reputation with your co-workers, friends, and other people important to you. If you've written a whole book about gambling with stolen money, will your supervisor be worried about you stealing from the company? If you tell the story of how you had multiple affairs with other people's husbands, will your friends continue to trust you?

On the upside, writing memoir has the potential to free you and your readers from the shame we so easily carry from having behaved in socially unacceptable ways. And furthermore, memoirs dealing with these sorts of subjects can possibly change our cultural dialogue. You can help others become more compassionate and less judgmental, and what an astounding thing to do!

EXERCISES

1. Write a scene in your memoir depicting what you consider your most embarrassing or shameful behavior. What does this scene illustrate for you? How would you feel about others reading it? How do you feel while reading it?

2. Write a scene in your memoir about the first time you engaged in bad behavior. Think about the circumstances of the scene. Who was present? Where were you? How did your relationships with the other characters and environment affect your behavior? How did your behavior affect those relationships?

3. Consider your poor behavior. Did you keep it a secret from others, or was it something generally accepted and shared by those around you? In what ways was the behavior fulfilling and damaging? What about this behavior made it worth continuing? What made it worth changing?

4. Write a scene in your memoir that illustrates a key moment of objectionable behavior. Imagine you're reading the memoir from the point of view of someone who doesn't know anything about the behavior. How does it feel to have that secret exposed? What would you include or remove to help draw your reader into the experience?

5. Read a memoir that focuses on addiction or some other harmful behavior. How does the author portray this experience? Does it feel sensationalized or underemphasized? Does she draw connections to possible reasons for her behavior or leave readers to make their own conclusions? Drawing on aspects of this memoir, write a scene where you attempt to balance the experience of the behavior with some insight into its roots.

SAVING MY LIFE
Sheila Hageman

One of the issues that came up repeatedly when I was getting my MFA in creative nonfiction from Hunter College, CUNY, was how to deal with writing about people who are still alive. My peers and I most often concluded that the truth was the most important ideal, that we must tell our stories, first and foremost, without thought of protecting people from our past. Of course, alongside that realization was the accepted legal and moral responsibility not to merely vent anger and exact retribution on people who had hurt us. Such writing never equaled compelling reading anyway.

It was all so easy and fun to imagine having this real-world dilemma in the future—that one day, with our memoirs about to be published, we would need to deal with that "truth" or "respect" predicament.

I had begun writing my memoir a long time before I began my graduate degree, back on the first day I set foot in a strip club at eighteen years old. At the time, I was writing only about myself and my experiences in the present. I was sure my tale about stripping would be a must-read because I thought that I was such a good writer and that the stripping world was titillating and unwritten about.

Years later, after many other stripper memoirs had already been published, I came to realize that having an interesting story was not enough to write a successful memoir. I began exploring the hows and whys of the story I had to tell, which of course brought me to my childhood. I delved into my memories of how I felt about my body and my value as a girl.

My writing became not so much a question of *what* happened to me as a little girl that lead me to become a stripper (although that was important, too) but how I *experienced* and *made sense* of what had happened to me as I was growing up that led me to make the choices I made as a young woman.

My parents' relationship, or lack thereof, had a lot to do with how I learned to see and value myself, but the turning point for me came when I was twelve and discovered my father's porno magazines in the basement. My parents had just divorced, and the porno trunk was the one thing my father had left behind when he moved out.

As an impressionable and naïve girl, those female images and everything they represented—sexiness, womanhood, and desirability—fed into my own development as a woman. I desired to be seen as a sexy woman because that's what I thought men valued and loved. And after a childhood of feeling invisible and unloved, being a porn woman held a beacon of hope for me.

My dad knew my story, that I had become a stripper and nude model at eighteen, but he had tried to ignore it over the years and never talked about it. Shortly before *Stripping Down: A Memoir* came out, I sat him down and gave him a quick overview of the book. I asked him if I could use his name; he said he'd rather I didn't, and I agreed not to.

It turns out that he had assumed that meant I was going to remove *him* from the book, not just his name. When the book was published, he saw in our town paper (where I live and he works) a story on the front page about the memoir, which he thought painted him in a negative way.

People were asking him if that was his daughter. He was mortified. And he saw a blurb for the book, which mentioned "my estranged father."

He saw what he thought was an attack on him and reacted. He came over to my house when only my husband, Nick, was there, and he was so angry that Nick thought he was going to have a heart attack, but he wouldn't tell Nick anything. My stepmother called me and could barely speak. All of the *How dare you do this to your father!*

Instead of being proud of me for searching out myself and my life, of trying to make sense of who I had been and who I had become, I was being attacked for writing my life. I wished my father would have read the book. He would have read my author's note on the first page.

> For all the people who live within the pages of this book, I thank you for being a part of my life. I have represented people and my life's events as honestly as I can as I remember them. Nothing I write is meant to hurt anyone; I tried to interpret myself, my motivations, my life. As a memoirist, I understand that people may remember events differently than I do, but I have done my best to remain true to my memory, which is all I can do and offer to the world.

When my father could finally speak to me on the phone, he went on the attack. He told me he'd never be able to forgive me or trust me again. He never wanted to see me again. The only time he wanted to hear from me was if there was an emergency with one of the kids.

I apologized and sobbed. *I didn't mean to hurt you.*

I felt as though I were being accused of something I'd worked so hard to avoid. I didn't feel the book was an attack on my father at all.

I kept asking my father, "Have you read the book? You'll see that although I talk about the hard stuff, the eventual outcome is that I forgive you. No, there isn't even anything to forgive. You were doing the best you could at the time. Just like I do now with my own children."

The book wasn't written about my father, but his paternal role meant that his story was necessarily entangled in my own life and story. I cannot tell the story of how I became who I am today without telling the story of where I came from.

A few months later, after he had gotten over his initial anger, we met for lunch. I'd been contacted by Dr. Phil; they wanted to fly my father and me out to be on the show. I tried to convince him to do it; it was a chance for us to get our frustrations out in the open and a chance for us to heal. And of course, as an author published by a small press, I knew an opportunity like that could make the difference for my book with publicity.

My father refused. I got other TV offers, but under the same requirements: only if my father would come on the show, too. And of course, he wouldn't.

There's been a slow "healing" over the years since the book's publication. Life has returned to something resembling the normality we had before the book. We visit on the holidays; we have the occasional dinner together.

The book is never spoken about, nor me as a writer. Never.

And for some reason that is how my family wishes for my story to remain. Unspoken. As many families feel, I imagine, the hard stuff, the unseemly things, are not meant to be discussed, let alone shared with the world.

But after growing up under that mentality and almost drowning in its quiet hold, I became something else. I became a person who needs to tell the story, to discuss the ramifications, to try to heal the past and protect the future.

I even believe that writing my life may have saved my life.

I broke free from an oppressive state of being and a culture that says we should just pretend everything is okay, even when it isn't; I stood up and looked at my life and shared with others in the hope of finally being heard and seen for my truth and possibly helping other women who felt they were not allowed to tell their truth.

I regret hurting my father unintentionally, but I do not and cannot regret telling my story; it is no exaggeration to say that my existence depends on my continually trying to figure out the meaning of my life. I owe this honesty not only to myself but to my daughter, too, so that she might feel free enough to talk about life as it happens to her, rather than waiting for many years to pass in the loneliness and pain that is the curse of holding ourselves silent.

Sheila Hageman is a mother of three and author of *Stripping Down: A Memoir*, a meditation on womanhood and body image. Her decision-making guide and self-discovery journal, *The Pole Position: Is Stripping for You? (And How to Stay Healthy Doing It)*, teaches women to value their identities by helping them understand their motivations for stripping. She received her MFA in creative writing from Hunter College, CUNY, where she also graduated as valedictorian with a BA in English. She is a yoga instructor and teaches writing at Housatonic Community College and the University of Bridgeport. To learn more about Sheila and everything she does, please visit sheilahageman.com or strippingdown.com.

THE AFTERWARD
Nicole Hardy

By the time I got heckled, I'd forgotten to be worried about it happening. My book-tour audiences had been so supportive, I'd allowed myself to let go of life's most essential truth: There are haters, and they are gonna hate.

The e-mails should've kept me wary—those blistering missives sent just hours after the essay that preceded my memoir hit *The New York Times* Internet site: *So let me get this straight. You can't find a Mormon who doesn't want kids or a non-Mormon who will marry a virgin? Not one? What's the "new" standard you've adopted? 3 dates first before sex? A handshake?*

I was expecting these vitriolic bombs, dropped casually into my e-mail in-box, and I'll admit to a perverse sort of joy in the irony: how often I was called a whore when in said essay I was a thirty-five-year-old virgin. But this moment—onstage in front of a packed audience in a community college theater—felt different. Decidedly un-joyful.

Here was a sixty-year-old woman, in real time, declaring loudly into a microphone, "Well I'm Mormon, and that wasn't *my* experience!" A sea of heads turned in unison to the upper left of the theater, wanting a face to connect to the outburst. Her heckling wasn't violent or profane. It was decidedly prim in comparison to the shoe throwing that's plagued some of our nations' leaders.

Still, the woman was indignant. Adamant. I sat onstage, stunned into a flashback by the tone of her voice. There I was, in my parents' living room, seven years prior, in the moment just after I'd told them I was leaving my religious practice. This woman's voice was an echo of my mother's—not her words but the fear that drove them. Feeling threatened, ambushed by my decision, my mother had spoken in the same panicked tenor: But we're supposed to be *together!*

Not only had I done this thing, but also—perhaps worse—I'd written about it. I'd written a memoir about God and sex and had said, truthfully, on those pages and in that theater and in venues across the country, that God didn't create me to be a mother. That

I'd never felt a maternal urge, which is about as close to blasphemy as a person can get in the construct of the Mormon Church.

The woman in the audience, like the people I love most in the world, subscribe to a brand of faith that depends not upon believing but upon *knowing* the one, complete truth. Absent of shadow, absent of doubt. So it didn't surprise me when she leaned closer to the mic, which was held by a fledgling, obviously uncomfortable theater tech, to announce, "I have a thirty-four-year-old daughter. And it wasn't *her* experience either!"

Based on my heckler's age now, it seemed fair to assume she married and had her daughter in her early twenties. About the same time my mother had me. So, no, my heckler's experience was not like mine. Nowhere near.

I tried to explain in a sentence or two the central conflicts of my memoir: that my commitment to abstinence before marriage made me undateable outside the church, where I was considered intriguing, eligible, attractive. And my broken biological clock made me undateable within it: someone who needed to try harder, pray harder, do better, be different so God would bless me with more righteous desires. I was an unmarriageable girl, waiting for marriage and caught in the vacuum of a middle place so isolating, so barren after so many years that it had the power to take my breath.

Did I understand, Nicole, [that] you made clear while dating that you did not want children? said one of the messages, illuminated on my laptop screen. *Thus you seem to be angry at a religion that values families so highly? I really need to think why you may see yourself as a victim of a culture where the vast majority of the men want children? ... you don't respect men in the culture that values children?*

Not wanting children equals anger. That's the most common conclusion. It equals rebellion, victimhood, and (somehow) a disrespect for men. Except it didn't. Doesn't. Even so, I don't doubt that ten years ago, I'd have reacted similarly to a woman writing a book about leaving the church. Such decisions should be private. Kept quiet. The publicity is harmful: It opens the door for the church to be judged and criticized, for viruses of misinformation to spread, for the retelling of tasteless jokes.

The woman in the theater wanted me to be quiet. To stop trampling what was sacred to her. What was perfect and right. The church is beloved by its members, in the same way people are—it is their truest love. Crimes against it, betrayals real or perceived, feel intimate. Feel personal and cruel. On both sides, which is why I imagine I know a bit about what it's like to get divorced, though I've never been married. I watched my life's partner turn, by imperceptible degrees, unrecognizable, and lose the capacity to love me, despite the years I spent trying to make it otherwise.

Hearing me say that would be unbearable for my heckler, I suspect. I can feel her cringe, even as I write the sentence. She needs me to have been the one who failed. Hence, the anger. The need to jump in and protect what is hers.

"Wasn't anyone *nice* to you?" she asks, as if a lack of niceness were the problem. It seems preposterous, this reduction. Until you realize that in order to preserve her experience, she must shrink mine to the size of a handful—make it small enough to toss aside.

In my snarkier fantasies, I snap back. Oh, my mistake, I didn't realize I was supposed to write *your* memoir. Or thanks for proving my point: that only one kind of female experience has value in the church. In my angrier fantasies, I tear her to pieces with words like shards of glass. But I know firsthand the danger that hovers when even the smallest thread comes loose. I know why she can't give an inch.

Still, I kept talking. Openly, about my desire for sex, my near-desperate craving for human contact: By my mid-thirties, a good-night kiss could turn dangerous in the space of thirty seconds, and I was terrified of ruining my life in that slice of time. I'd held it so high for so long—the commitment I made, the golden-hued promises behind it—even as the weight of it was breaking me.

I tried to explain it to her: the complicated, perpetual conflicts of identity, the doctrine of marriage and motherhood, the habitual infantilization I experienced. "I'll speak to you as I'd speak to my daughter," say the letters. No, I write back. Speak to me like a contemporary, since that's what we are.

"I feel sad for you," the heckler said, finally. "That you felt you had to leave because people were mean." And there it was, my head beating against the same brick wall of mean/nice, right/wrong, obedient/rebellious.

But as a writer of memoir—of this particular memoir—I signed up for this. I talked about the thing I was least allowed to talk about, revealed my most vulnerable self, gave people the stones and sticks to throw.

"We need to do better for our people," one woman wrote. "We need to be more embracing of diversity, more perceptive of individual needs, more loving, less judgmental." And in the next sentence: "I pray for you … I know your happiness is illusory."

I signed up for that, too: for the condescension and the name-calling, the ugly and the slut and the sellout and the whore and the bitch and the closeted and the you'll burn and the you deserve. Why would I do it? My mother asked the question, just before my book went to print. Why would I *want* to?

I sat across from her at her kitchen table with a manuscript in my hand, asking permission to publish what I'd already written, what might have already been too late to change. Could she live with these three sentences outlining the abuses of her childhood? I held out a piece of paper, but she wouldn't take it. "Just read it to me," she said, with her hands over her eyes. "Read it again," she said, but it wasn't until the third or fourth round that she let the words seep in enough to process them. By then, both of us were spent with weeping.

Why would you do this, she asked about the writing. I didn't have an answer until later—an epiphany buried in the script of a two- or three-star Julia Roberts movie. The scene when a group of reluctant, reactive art students at Wellesley are asked to stand in front of a Jackson Pollock painting. It's a diversion that threatens their sensibility, that they can't or don't want to understand. "Stop talking, and look," says the Julia Roberts character. It's the thing I'd like to say to my heckler. I'd say it as kindly as I could.

"You're not required to write a paper. You're not even required to like it. You *are* required to consider it."

It's not just me, I'd like to tell her. Consider the woman at the restaurant where I work, who, when I asked if she was ready to order, looked up at me with the most naked expression. "I divorced my husband after ten years because I could no longer pretend I wasn't gay," she told me, having just read my story. "He told everyone, all our friends, that I was mentally ill. He tried to take our children. My father said I was failing ..." She paused, as if to summon courage. "My father told me I was failing at life. My parents didn't speak to me for fifteen years."

Consider the woman eyeing me from across the dining room. A different woman, a different night. She shook her head when I apologized for keeping her waiting. She looked at me for a long time without speaking, turned her back to her husband, her in-laws, and her son. I knelt on the concrete floor, trying to hear over the clatter of plates, the Beatles on the stereo. "I came here because of you," she said, reaching for my hand, holding it in both of hers.

"I left the church in my thirties," she said, and told me about her struggle to remain celibate. The desperation, the loneliness that mounted as she got older and remained single. She wanted a Mormon life, an eternal marriage, children. "I *tried*," she tells me, "I promise. I tried." Her eyes shone with tears. "I just couldn't do it; I couldn't stand to be so alone." She was excommunicated ten years prior, she said, holding her hand over her stomach, as if it ached. "Ten years and I'm still grieving."

"But look now," I said, glancing at her family. Not quite knowing what to say.

"I thank God every day that I found this man who loves me. And that I was still able to have a child. But no one understands how you can destroy your family in the leaving. How abandoned you feel when you don't get the life you were promised—when what you're offered instead is a life you simply cannot live."

I stood to let one of my co-workers pass behind me with an armful of plates. The woman stood, too, and put her arms around me, as if we were sisters rather than strangers. "My husband keeps asking, 'Aren't I happy for you? How can I be happy, when I know your sadness?'"

Consider the other letters—hundreds reaching, repeating the same refrains, notes, like a choir in a round saying, I have struggled   so painful and

    an outsider not belonging always like such

        I can't

they don't but stay   anyway

because of fear

or

        family   conflicted I

connect will I

being loved   I'm not   alone feeling

    give me   some

treasure some

     restore   cathartic and

                          courage

     reveal   of your should not

anguish what purpose

my heart and her   should

         ached

         kicked out   the easiest

was me gone   so starved for   how many

    ways what cannot

        be said

         of home affection and touch

      that I

desperate

      I broke   when you

              cried to write what

              cannot   said the pain

I am none of theirs

though

we lived   parallel   speechless

and the solace in
thank you

glorious divine   is opposite, is almost
                        only thank you

for loved for listening for actually
for the first for the

    I have that with you   as well
                                        I knew I never

        I used to
        I was the only
    and about the despair
                being lifted
reminded
    I hope less alone
for the time I was   and vulnerable
I could pore over the secretly
            I don't know
            the ending   the normal

    yet   like you other like us unlike

and I wanted   I know you
I sobbed
with a voice   to you

Nicole Hardy's *Confessions of a Latter-Day Virgin: A Memoir* was
published in the United States and abroad in 2013. Her nonfiction
has appeared in literary journals and newspapers including *The*

New York Times and was selected as "notable" in *Best American Essays 2012*. Her poetry collections include *This Blonde* and *Mud Flap Girl's XX Guide to Facial Profiling*—a chapbook of pop culture–inspired sonnets. Visit her at nicolehardy.com.

HE, HIM, HIS
Janet W. Hardy

Over the breakfast I'd paid for, I asked the question that I hoped would justify the expense: "Can you tell me what stuff I should steer clear of mentioning when I write about you?"

And the cost of a plate of eggs and bacon disappeared down the drain when I heard the answer I most feared: "You're just going to have to show me the draft, and I'll tell you what to take out."

The man across the table had been my live-in partner, lover, business associate, and co-collaborator for thirteen years. I knew he had never really forgiven me for leaving him. I also knew that the first thing he'd done after our breakup was to get himself an apartment next door to the law school he was about to begin attending.

By the time we sat across from each other nearly a decade later, sipping weak coffee in a San Francisco greasy spoon, he'd passed the bar exam, although he didn't yet have a license to practice. But even if he didn't have a certificate hanging on his wall, he had the adversarial temperament of an attorney. During our split, he'd threatened me several times with legal action over how our money and possessions were divided. And I'd heard that he'd threatened some of his other lovers with invasion-of-privacy suits when they posted what seemed to him like too much information about their bedroom activities. He also lectured local business owners on the civil and legal consequences of whichever of their policies he didn't agree with.

But I was stuck. He was an essential character in the story of my ascent from a fairly ordinary teenage girl who liked to think about spanking to an internationally respected BDSM (bondage/discipline, dominance/submission, sadomasochism) educator and the crash-and-burn that had ended my sex life and sent me to live in celibacy in a small Oregon town.

For many years, this man and I had been arguably the most famous kinky heterosexual couple in the United States. Each of us had written several well-respected how-to books about bondage, spanking, and so on; we'd traveled together and separately all around the country to teach workshops, sell books, and make friends.

I'd learned a good portion of what I knew about kink from him. He was the first person I'd fallen in love with while doing BDSM. He'd cofounded the small publishing company that issued our books, although he later sold his share to me. I had been the First Lady of heterosexual kink and he'd been the President, and there was no way I was going to disguise him.

As I wrote the first 20,000 words of my story, I was elated with how fluidly and wittily the words were flowing. And then I got to the chapter where I attended my first kink gathering in San Francisco—the gathering where I met a tall, bespectacled guy who'd been laboring over a how-to-do-kink manuscript for several years—and I stopped dead.

I couldn't write my book without him in it, and he wouldn't let me write it with him in it. Every neuron in my brain told me that the scenes he and I had done together—those profound, life-altering, ecstatic, messy, spectacular scenes—were essential to my story. And every day of the life I'd lived with him, everything I knew about him, told me he'd never, ever, ever give me permission to publish them.

By legal standards—the person being described must be readily identifiable to the reader—there was no way I was going to get away with changing his name, making him a brunet instead of an ash blond, or even changing his gender. And by privacy standards, pretty much everything we'd done would strike a jury as an "offensive act," the other criterion for invasion of privacy (in spite of the fact that we'd spent years trying to convince the world that there was nothing offensive in consensual and hotly desired BDSM).

In other words, I was screwed.

"Can you write it as fiction?" one friend asked.

"Nobody would believe it," I replied.

But could I compromise? Sweating, I began a rewrite in which I added a new, fictional character—another lover whom I'd met early in my BDSM life. It was barely possible; everybody knew that my relationship with my ex had been an open one, that we'd had other lovers, both committed and casual throughout our years together. Who was to say that I couldn't have had a long-term guy on the side? If I wrote him as a married man, that would explain why nobody had met him. I could give the fake man all the fights and quirks and embarrassing stuff that I knew had the potential to land me in court.

But the words were coming slowly and badly, each one hard and tight. All the loose, easy flow of the first 20,000 words of text withered up and turned into the writerly analog of acute constipation. I am a bad fiction writer and a worse liar, and as I lay awake every night trying to figure a way through my impasse, I knew this book was not going to get written.

Fortunately I'd done one thing right, back when I thought it was all going to be easy. I'd booked trips to two different writing conferences—the San Francisco Writers Conference and the Association of Writers and Writing Programs (AWP) gathering—which took place within a few weeks of one another. (I couldn't really afford to do both conferences, but back when the writing was easy, I had figured I'd find an agent and/or a publisher at one of them and the advance would more than pay my expenses. Ha, ha.)

The two gatherings couldn't be more different. San Francisco is all about the mainstream publishing track. There are agent speed-dating events and ask-the-publisher events and lots of optimistic talk about advances and author tours. I signed up for all of them, honed my "elevator pitch" ("I'm writing a book about the twenty years I spent as one of the world's premier educators on sadomasochism and polyamory, including the episode so frightening that I haven't done S/M or had sex since"), and began talking.

And one after another excruciatingly well-groomed New York editor and agent looked at me like I was from another planet. (Well, perhaps I was.) But the upshot was, to use one woman's words, "Oh, my. That is ... quite a story. But I wouldn't have any idea what to do with a book like that."

Thank the writing deities for AWP, just a few weeks later in Seattle. AWP, which takes place in a different city every year, is the touch point for creative writing programs around the world. Compared to San Francisco, it is much more about the academic and literary aspects of writing and publishing.

For example, the very first workshop I attended was a panel of writers espousing the idea that creative nonfiction was an inherently queer genre. Each of them had written and was performing what was essentially a prose poem about the odd mix of interiority and narrative, confession and poetry, that constitutes the personal essay or literary memoir. When one of them cited Shel Silverstein, I knew I'd come home.

The event went on strengthening my conviction that I was in the right place. Even a very tedious presentation about mind-mapping software made a solution click into place: If I had a mind map, I wouldn't have to go downstairs and wallow in a hot bath every time I couldn't figure out what should happen next—I'd be able to refer to the map! (It's been two months now, and I can attest that mind mapping works.)

Late in the afternoon on the last day of the conference, I attended a workshop about the role of university and independent presses in the world of publishing. One after another of the panelists said the same thing, and it wasn't "I wouldn't know what to do with a book like that." It was, instead, "University and independent presses are the proper home for books that don't fit into conventional narrative forms and subject categories but that offer significant literary quality and unique viewpoints."

Well!

I left after that; I'd heard what I needed to hear. On the six-hour train ride back home, I scrawled in my Moleskine, feeling the skeleton of my book dissolving and reshaping, dictated not by the first-this-then-that chronology of my life but by a more essential through-line: a lifelong desire for intensity so annihilating that it dissolves the ego and the culmination in which I quenched that desire.

Suddenly the book was driven not by time but by fantasy and experience: the fantasies of punishment, redemption, and catharsis that had steered my life since earliest childhood and the amazing, transformative scenes that had shaped me.

The book now opens with one of those fantasies, so embarrassing to reveal that I tend to skip over that page when I'm editing (and which I'm certainly not going to include here). The fantasy is followed by the passage below.

> I used generic words for the participants in this fantasy because I rarely make up my own people. Instead, I use people made up by other writers: Jean-Luc Picard and Q, Batman and the Riddler, Captain Robinson and Dr. Smith—well, you get the idea. If I wrote the fantasy using those people, it would be fan fiction and nobody would publish it because those people are owned by the person who invented them or the company that publishes them. … However, I spent thirty years of my life doing my best to make my fantasies real, and I used real people for that. I don't own those people either, so I'll use generic words for them, too.

And it's that simple: he, him, his. It doesn't matter which of those scenes took place with my recalcitrant ex and which with the dozens of men, women, and others with whom I've shared my darkest and sweetest desires. The story is an internal one, not an external one, so no name but mine matters.

The book is back on track, although it's requiring me to reach a lot deeper and reveal things that are a lot scarier. But I think it's going to work.

And I don't intend to show it to him at all.

Janet W. Hardy is the founder of Greenery Press and the author or co-author of eleven books about alternative sexualities, including *The Ethical Slut: A Practical Guide to Polyamory, Open Relationships & Other Adventures* and *Girlfag: A Life Told in Sex and Musicals*. She is hard at work on an as-yet-untitled memoir about her years as a globe-trotting BDSM practitioner and educator, and the dramatic culmination that brought an end to her kink and sex practices. She lives, writes, and bakes in Eugene, Oregon, with her spouse, dogs, cat, and chickens.

CHAPTER SIX

just between us

SECRET TELLING

In one of my favorite memoirs, *Because I Remember Terror, Father, I Remember You*, Sue William Silverman reveals the long-buried family secret that she was sexually molested by her father from age five to eighteen. She started writing the memoir shortly after both her parents had died, and she was aware that it would expose her father, who was a high-ranking government official and banker, and that he would be unable to defend himself. Why would Silverman have risked her father's reputation? Some might think she was after revenge. This may very well be the truth here. Child molesters often tell their victims that they should never tell others about the molestation. By exposing her father's behavior, she ends a harmful silence, and this is certainly part of her intention. But I don't believe she was aiming to smear his name or to finally show people who he really was. When you read the poetic sentences, when you follow the emotional finesse of her experiences, you know that isn't the case. Rather, as the excerpt below indicates, Silverman wants to be freed from her secret's constraints.

> [I]t's a relief to no longer hide behind a veil of secrets. Growing up, I lived a double life. On the face of it, we seemed like a normal, happy family. My father had an important career, first in government, then in banking. Nice houses. Pretty clothes. But all this seeming perfection was a veneer, a facade, for the *other* life. It masked the reality that my father sexually molested me, a reality never spoken aloud either in private in our house or in public.[1]

When you expose secrets, it's easy to feel like a tattletale. It would be easier, it seems sometimes, to stay silent, to allow the lies to continue. Sometimes telling secrets can feel like it will kill you or will blow your family to bits because the secrets and lies formed the structure and foundation on which your life—on which all your family members' lives—were built.

If you are a woman, this pressure might be even stronger. It was Tillie Olsen in *Silences* who noted that "women are traditionally trained to place others' needs first, to feel these needs as their own." Indeed, when one approaches life this way, she lives with the illusion that others' needs are her own needs, and so to write about

---

1 Sue William Silverman, *Fearless Confessions: A Writer's Guide to Memoir* (Georgia: University of Georgia Press, 2009).

secrets is to betray not only the family but your entire sense of self. Heavy stuff, right?

Yet if you don't share your secrets in writing, it is almost impossible for readers to connect intimately with your story. Think of it in relation to an affair. It was the family therapist Frank Pittman in *Private Lies: Infidelity and the Betrayal of Intimacy* who wrote that in an affair the issue is less with the person with whom one lies and more about whom one lies *to*. He notes that the person with whom you have secrets is the one with whom you'll feel more connected, more intimate. And you will feel uncomfortable with the one from whom you're keeping truths. If we apply this to memoir, your reader will not feel close to you if you hide behind a veil, and as I emphasize again and again in this book, it is the readers' relationship with your story that matters most. In *Telling Secrets: A Memoir*, Frederick Buechner sheds light on the significance of secrets.

> ... [secrets] tell what is perhaps the central paradox of our condition—that what we hunger for perhaps more than anything else is to be known in our full humanness, and yet that is often just what we also fear more than anything else.

If indeed we read memoir to see ourselves more clearly, if we write memoir in order to know ourselves, then secret telling is an essential part of our work. It always will be. I would argue that you cannot write a memoir without divulging secrets. Patricia Hampl calls memoir writing "a hunger for the world." That is exactly what it feels like, doesn't it? A voracious desire for more connection, more you, more me, more truth.

HOW TO WRITE ABOUT SECRETS

In the following passage, Sue William Silverman explains how she motivates her students to open up about themselves in their writing.

I teach creative nonfiction at Vermont College of Fine Arts, and sometimes I'll have a student who feels paralyzed about writing family secrets. So I remind my students that they've already lived through the dark, scary time. That's in the past. Now it's a matter of putting it down on paper, and now they have a support system to help them if they get scared: They have their fellow writers, their faculty mentors, friends, and so on. In short, they are not alone. So I tell them just to focus on one word at a time … then one sentence, then a paragraph, then a page … and soon they'll have a complete manuscript. But basically, in this moment, all you need to do is write one word.

All you need to do is write one word. All you have to do is write the next word and then the next. Initially, that really is all you have to do. The anxiety you might have about divulging secrets is irrelevant if you don't ever write the book or the essay, so write it. Write it anyway. The writing itself is a kind of courageousness that helps you transcend those secrets that controlled you. The page is safe. The people who give you feedback—mentors, peers, and friends—are safe. No one here will shame you. No one will tell you not to tell the truth. Just get the words down, each one a footstep across the vast desert of secrets that tries to paralyze you.

So how do you write about secrets? You just do it. You write. Because if you don't, you may always wish you had. Victoria Loustalot wrote about how her father kept his homosexuality a secret for years, and her grandparents were upset that she included the secret in her book.

> I wrote the book I needed to write. I knew there was a chance they wouldn't understand, and they don't. I don't think they ever will, frankly. I want to live an open and honest life. A life in which love and acceptance are the

foundation for all of my relationships. And that's what this book is. That's what it's about: honesty and acceptance. I feel awful that I hurt my grandparents, but I was tired of the secrets. The secrets stop with my dad's generation. I just won't do it.

Secrets often lead to the memoir you *need* to write. Consider *The Kiss* by Kathryn Harrison or *House Rules: A Memoir* by Rachel Sontag. Both books are about the secret worlds that existed behind the closed doors of childhood and young adulthood. Had they not written their secrets, a different truth might have ruled their lives, one that wasn't true for them and was therefore harmful to their psyches. Jillian Lauren comments below on the cathartic benefits of memoir writing.

> It's a cliché, but my experience was that the truth did indeed set me free. It set me free to be myself and not run from my past. In fact, it was such a great experience that now I'm hooked on writing from my life. The experience of creating narrative out of the events of my life has been tremendously rewarding and liberating for me, even on a small scale.

When you write about the confusion that secrets cause, you make something amorphous and terrifying into something understandable. Keeping silent about secrets doesn't make them go away. Instead they grow monstrous, less understandable, and even more frightening.

Consider, too, that telling your secrets may save someone else from harm. While Gigi Little does obsess over the possibility of hurting someone when she writes a memoir, she has come to the realization that the importance of her work extends well beyond her own life.

> [T]hat essay on my computer screen turns into an essay in a book or a journal, and my neuroses let go. I see it in print, and the story becomes less about what I'm saying

about my life and the people in it and more about what
the reader finds in it about hers.

I noted in chapter one that memoir is bound more to the reader than
the writer. It's the reader who must see herself in your words, who
must have a relationship with your story that will transform her in
some way. Releasing your secret will surely release someone else's. It
may give your readers the courage to face their own painful truths, to
speak out, and to change their own narratives. Sue William Silverman
had this experience.

> What means the most to me are the e-mails I receive
> from hundreds of people who thank me for, in effect,
> writing their story, too. Many people thank me for my
> books, telling me that, because of them, they don't feel
> as alone. They now know they are not the only ones
> struggling to recover from incest or sexual addiction.
> Always, this will be more important to me than possibly
> upsetting family or friends. I'm willing to risk the loss
> of friendship, risk relationships with family members …
> risk anything in order to be able to write my narratives.
> I am a writer. Nothing can change this.

Kim Barnes found that revealing family secrets freed her father as well.
Before writing *In the Wilderness*, her father had shunned her. While
she wrote, however, they began to discuss the book's details. She said
that by allowing herself to be flawed, vulnerable, and compassionate,
her father felt the desire to be as well. He told her he didn't *want* her
to publish those secrets, but he believed she should anyway. It was a
great gift for Barnes.

EXERCISES

1. As discussed in this chapter, there are many reasons to confess our secrets in memoirs. Why do you feel compelled to write and share your secrets? Briefly discuss your personal, interpersonal, and any larger societal motivations for exposing your secrets.

2. Write three of your biggest secrets on a piece of paper. What happens inside you? What would it feel like if your mother read them? Your best friend? A whole bunch of strangers?

3. Consider your biggest secret. What motivated you to keep the information secret? Was it a family secret that you'd kept since childhood? Was this secret part of your identity, or did it threaten your identity? Did it keep others at a distance or draw them closer to you? Write a scene that illustrates how your biggest secret affected you and your relationships with others.

4. Write a list of others' secrets that you discuss in your memoir. How are these secrets important to your narrative? How can you protect these people's identities without leaving out vital parts of your narrative?

5. Write a list of things that your secrets have protected you from and a list of ways your secrets have inhibited you. What have you sacrificed in order to keep your secrets?

6. Write a scene in your memoir that shows how your secrets directly affected a close relationship. What were the unspoken fears you had? How may confessing those secrets have affected the relationship then? How might confessing those secrets affect that relationship now?

THE RIGHT TO WRITE
Erica Rivera

"I don't like my character," my mother said sternly as she stood in my doorway.

Almost five years had passed since I published my first memoir, *Insatiable: A Young Mother's Struggle with Anorexia*. My mother was still upset about it.

I wrote the book during a dark time in my life. I was newly divorced, recovering from an eating disorder that could have killed me, and living in my mother's basement. When I penned the manuscript, I had no idea a publisher would buy it. But Berkley Books, an imprint of Penguin, did. And as the publishing date loomed, my mother became more and more incensed by the idea that she was being written about.

Not that she would ever say so.

My family doesn't really "do" emotions, much less have upfront, honest conversations. To wit: One night, I came home to find my mother had left a stack of photo albums in my room.

"I found those old photo albums," she told me the next day over lunch.

Found? I wondered. They weren't exactly missing. They'd been in her closets for years.

"So you can get ideas of other things to write about," she said.

***

Before my mother had even read a page of the memoir, she threatened to sue me.

"If the goal is to get me out of your basement," I told her, "suing me doesn't make much sense."

I was caring for two preschool-aged daughters and hadn't been employed full-time since before they were born. The book advance was big enough to last me at least two years. How could I say no to that?

Finances aside, I *wanted* to publish the book. I had conquered my fiercest demons. I deserved to tell my story, and I believed in doing so unflinchingly. Besides, if anyone was going to look bad in *Insatiable*, it was *me*. I wasted years as an anorexic shirking responsibility, acting slightly insane, and sacrificing my and my daughters' quality of life in the interest of fitting into size 0 jeans.

I had been told, after an early read by a professor, that the narrator was "mean." ("It's a memoir," I wanted to say. "The narrator is *me*!") My eating disorder had made me selfish, self-absorbed, shallow, and cold. I may have come out on top, but not before I hit rock bottom—hard. And every step of the way was told in excruciating detail in the memoir.

My mother played a bit part in the book. Due to her own battle with depression, a divorce from my father, and a breast cancer diagnosis when I was in my teens, I always felt that while she was physically present in my life, she wasn't "there" in any meaningful way. Those circumstances were part of my story, and they helped explain why I fell so far down the rabbit hole when confronted with adulthood.

Over the course of readying *Insatiable* for publication, my mother occasionally commented that she didn't like that I was "writing nasty things about me while you're living in my house."

The latter part of her complaint was resolved when, upon receiving the first third of my advance, I moved out. But the nastiness didn't stop, whether I wanted it to or not.

"We need more of your mother in here," my editor said after reading what I thought was the final draft of *Insatiable*. "There seems to be tension between you two, but I don't understand why."

That might have been because I'd left out a crucial event in our mother-daughter history: the night my mother attempted suicide. It was around Valentine's Day, 1999. I was seventeen. My stepfather was out of town, and my mother was apparently in so much psychological pain that she took to her bed and swallowed who knows how many pills.

For some reason—call it daughterly instinct—I knocked on her bedroom door to say "good night." When she didn't answer and I realized the door was locked, I broke in to find her unconscious. There was an envelope with my name on it propped on the dresser. In an instant, I recognized what was happening and called 9-1-1. The paramedics later told me I saved her life.

But I'd left that story out of *Insatiable*. It was nobody's business, right? Except it was, because I was writing a memoir and the omission was glaring.

So I put it in. My editor was pleased. (We are all whores when the price is right.)

***

In the weeks leading up to the pub date, my mother again expressed concern that I was raking her over the coals in the book, though she still hadn't read any of it. I told her that whatever she was imagining was likely far worse than what I had written.

"And if you don't like it, you're free to write a book of your own," I said.

"I don't have time for that," she spat back.

When *Insatiable* was released, I gave my mother a hardcover copy. In the dedication, I thanked her and my stepfather for putting up with me for so long. My mother e-mailed me to say my stepfather cried when he read that. She told me that he was reading the book aloud to her but editing out the upsetting parts (which I assumed meant anything about her). "So far your book is very well written and very good" was the extent of her reaction.

I shouldn't have been surprised that the rest of my family didn't really react at all. My father and my younger brother may have said, "Congratulations," but I don't remember much beyond them attending the release party.

My therapist, who was featured extensively in the book, was one of my most eager readers. "I smiled, laughed, and cried because it was so well written, fun to read, and also very sad at times," she told me when she finished. The clinic where I received treatment even reviewed *Insatiable* for its newsletter.

The boyfriend that had proposed to me and then reneged in the pages of *Insatiable* e-mailed me to say that while he was impressed I was publishing a book, he didn't appreciate my mass e-mail "pitching" it to all my contacts.

"Telling me your book is coming out is fabulous," he said. "Telling me to order it is kinda like the celebrity asking the crowd to cheer." Perhaps it's better he didn't buy a copy—he wouldn't have liked how I depicted him.

I also sent a copy of the book to a friend-with-benefits, who took part in a fling that I included in *Insatiable*.

"I *really* enjoyed your book and am very proud of you!" he told me after reading it. "Thanks for treating me kindly/fairly."

***

Insatiable received a modest amount of press during its first month on the market. Then it felt like the world forgot—except my mother, apparently, who was still thinking about it all these years later when she made her statement, apropos of nothing, in the doorway of my home.

For me, anorexia, single motherhood, *Insatiable*—all those things felt like a lifetime ago. The person who wrote that book is different than the person I am now. I'm remarried. I have stepchildren. I own a home. I'm a freelance writer and (gulp) a grown-up.

My mother is different, too. Whatever I lacked from her when I was a child—attention, affection, involvement—she is providing now, as the grandmother of my daughters.

I'd moved on. I'd assumed she had, too.

"It's kind of late to change anything now," I told her.

We haven't spoken about it since.

Looking back, I see *Insatiable* as a mixed blessing. If I were to do it all again, I would definitely write it. I don't know, however, that I would publish it. What I originally wrote and what ended up in bookstores are two different stories; the latter was processed, shaped to fit a particular market. At times, I compromised on its content because I didn't know I could stand up to my editor.

Ultimately *Insatiable* didn't change the way I write about people. Relationships are what excite me and make me feel alive; to eliminate others from my writing out of fear for their reactions would make for page after page of navel-gazing. Like a documentary photographer, I don't edit things out just because they're ugly. I put it all in. But does that need to be published? I don't know.

People in my life are well aware that anything they say or do can and may be used in a piece of my writing. It has prevented some from getting too close. It has caused others to preface conversations with "You can't write about this!" (And if they make that request, I honor it.)

If I were to publish *Insatiable* again, I'd like to think I'd be more compassionate, not just with my mother but with everyone involved. I'd like to think I wouldn't bow to my publisher's demands that I include every gory detail just for the shock factor. But maybe

I'd write it with the same brutal honesty, because if I wrote it with eyes of kindness, I doubt it would be as powerful.

My eating-disordered past is no longer a gaping, raw wound for me. It's a scar, and a barely visible one at that. But sometimes showing the wound and telling the story is what's necessary for it to heal. And if that makes my mother mad, so be it. She has her own stories to tell.

Erica Rivera is the author of *Insatiable: A Young Mother's Struggle with Anorexia* (Berkley/Penguin, 2009). She currently interviews small business owners for *Minnesota Business* magazine and writes entertainment features on a freelance basis for *Vita.mn.* Her writing has also appeared in *New York* magazine, *USA Today*, the *Star Tribune*, *Minnesota Meetings + Events* magazine, *Metromix*, and *The Daily Meal* as well as multiple anthologies. She lives in Minnesota with her family. Visit her website at www.ericarivera.net.

MY VERSION OF OUR STORY
Alyssa Royse

The idea that anything in our lives is completely private is something that makes no sense to me, in a life that is lived with others. As deeply intimate as the stories of our lives are to us, and as much as we see ourselves as their lone star, we are never the only characters in them. We are each the stars of our own versions of the stories we live with others. Two—or more—characters living the same events from wildly different perspectives, with different morals, different motives, different lessons, different endings. In my version I may be a romantic savior. In someone else's, a treacherous shrew. Though the events are the same, the casting and directing is inherently different.

The moment that we engage with others, we become characters in their story. Our story becomes theirs. Forever. There is no delete button for impressions left on the lives of others. You can't take them back or even stake a claim.

This, of course, is the hazard of loving—or even knowing—writers.

For two years, I dated a married man. When it began, I was trying to save my own marriage by exploring an open relationship. My husband and I agreed on this; I was honest about everything. Perhaps intrigued by this, the married man told me that he and his wife were separated and that they also had "an agreement." I didn't ask for more details; instead, I interpreted his words as if they fit into my story, not fully taking into account his story or his motives. Or those of his wife.

He was extraordinarily wealthy; I didn't bat an eye at the fact that his wife was in India or California for months at a time. I took it as proof that they were, indeed, living separate lives, trying to sort things out.

It never occurred to me that he was lying to me. That he was simply having an affair with me. As such, I respected his space when his wife was in town. Even as my husband and I officially declared an end to our marriage, we were still close, sharing friends and family alike. So I never batted an eye when my married man and his wife did the same. Or when they invited me to small social gatherings. I thought we were sharing a civilized open relationship.

Almost a year into it, I found out that his wife believed they were working on their marriage, trying to save it. That the times he had introduced us were not honesty but "hiding in plain sight."

His deliberate lack of specificity allowed him to lie indirectly, a fact I was reminded of on many occasions.

I was in love by the time I found out that his wife knew nothing of me and had not sanctioned other relationships. I spent another year with him. It was an emotionally brutal and grueling year in which everything I believed about myself—what I would do, what I believed, what I valued—was challenged. I saw sides of myself I never would have guessed existed. Anger like a natural disaster. Patience like a February blossom. Blind determination to not have been wrong about him or us, like a religious zealot. I believed that my pain made me a martyr for something I believed in, a love against all odds. I told myself that he was harmed and in pain and that my love could heal him and soothe him. I let myself believe I had that kind of power. It's the magical thinking of every mistress ever: *I am different.*

I wasted a second year in order to prove that I had not wasted the first.

When we finally broke up, in a protracted rage that I am surprised landed no one in jail or the hospital, I commented that I had learned so much and that ultimately it would benefit many. The many realities of magical thinking and delusional decisions became fascinating to me and seemed rich with wisdom and lessons that I couldn't wait to share.

I am a writer after all, a screenwriter specifically. I had begun writing a TV show about people in their forties going through changes like this. It is hysterical, painful, and injected with the kind of wisdom that hardship rapes into you.

He told me that I couldn't write anything that could in any way look anything like our story. That it wasn't my story to tell—it was his. His. Not mine.

No, I assured him. It's my story to tell, to do anything I want with. He was horrified. People would know that he had an affair.

(Mind you, everyone who knew us had already figured it out, even if it was never discussed.) I assured him that it was not my job to protect him from the repercussions of his actions. If he didn't want people to find out that he did things, the best strategy was not to do those things. Hoping no one will tell is a fool's strategy.

"It's my story, too," I told him, "You don't have exclusive rights to my story." I laughed when I said that, as we both come from film and theater, a world in which rights to stories are indeed bought and sold. I told him that he was welcome to make me an offer on the exclusive rights to my story.

He did not meet that with a sense of humor. Or an offer. (Not that I would have accepted one. My story is not for sale to anyone.)

But it did make things clear to me. Your story is yours. Common courtesy dictates that we protect the innocent but that we are not responsible for protecting people from the consequences of their own actions. My story is mine to do with as I please. And for the most part, telling it is what pleases me. Because what's the point of it all if we don't learn and grow? And isn't it all the better if we can help others learn and grow as well?

I am often asked where the lines are. What parts of our story do we have the right to tell, and when do we know? People believe that I tell all. While that may be the safest way to live your life in general—assuming that everyone will find out anyway and acting accordingly—that couldn't be further from the truth, really.

Of course there are rules. My rules are fairly simple.

1. Did it happen to me, with me, or because of me? If no, then I have no right to tell it. Stories that other people tell me about their lives are not mine to tell. If something about a story speaks to a larger truth and I think it can illustrate that truth, then I either ask the person who told it

for permission or rearrange the facts into an anonymous oblivion, rendering it a parable.

2. Did it happen to me but has no bearing on the world around me or humanity in general? Then I'm probably not going to discuss it in any way other than with the broadest strokes. As a sex and relationship writer, this is actually a very clear line for me. Though my writing will expose a general lust for sex and an exuberant contentment with my sex life, I will not discuss the details. Because they don't matter and because my husband does not want his sex life discussed. I am open and candid about loving sex because that is something that I think the world needs more of in order to heal generalized sexual shame. But no one needs to know the details of my—or anyone's—sex life.

3. Did it happen to me and have larger meaning that others can learn from but involves other people who have done no wrong and harm and doesn't need to be examined by others? I will go to great pains, for the most part, to protect those who I see as "innocent" actors in their own lives. I might share it but with an open hand rather than a pointed finger.

4. Then there are the stories, like the one of the affair that I truly didn't know I was having. A story so rich with questions that I can't help but explore it. I still ponder how I, someone who values truth above all else, could play that part in a story. I had to ask. I still do. I want to ask others. I want to create a space in which husbands and wives and boyfriends and girlfriends can all ask why. Why do we do this to each other? Why do we justify to the point of delusion? Why do we compromise what we believe about ourselves? Why do we lie, cheat, and deceive ourselves

and others? It's a story as old as humanity, one that never causes anything but pain, yet we still do it.

I'll not use his name, ever; it serves no purpose. But those who knew us both will know who it is, and that's okay with me. For all I know my writing will help heal both him and his wife—trauma often does that. Maybe it will stop others from making the same mistake—with him or with others. I will feel better knowing that I issued a warning about infidelity in general.

He didn't want me to tell my story because he didn't like the way it made his character look. He didn't want to be seen as that cliché of a guy—middle-aged, cheating on his wife. I didn't want to be that woman sleeping with someone else's husband. But I was. I think he hated himself for what he did. It's a guess. It's just a guess based on my believing that, under it all, he was a decent person who got lost and confused and did the wrong thing.

I might think that, however, because that's what I was. And because believing he was truly bad would make it even worse for me. I might have to believe there was something good in there in order to believe there was some magical and vague justification for the fact that I stayed even after I knew.

It doesn't make me look good either. But beyond good and bad, there is simple humanity. I don't fear this truth, because I have never presented myself as anything other than human. As flawed, prone to making mistakes. Being scared and imperfect as a character is part of the story I have always told myself and, just as important, others.

I don't really know what his motives were. I don't know what his story is. I don't know what part I play in his version. I owe you, the readers, that truth: The only person I can speak for is me.

Beyond this little piece here, I still have not told the story. I am still working on the TV show, and I am proud of it. It is excellent. It doesn't point to him specifically, just men like him, and there are many. And to women like me, of whom there are many. And we often switch roles—infidelity knows no gender. I will explore the story because the story of what we do to find joy and peace, to cause harm and rebuild, is the only story that interests me. In all its forms.

To not tell it was hurting me. To deny myself my story in order to protect him makes no sense.

After all, the minute he wrote me into his story, he became a character in mine.

Our lives are not monologues or soliloquies. Our characters are interpreted by others. It is best to live accordingly. The consequences of your actions are your own.

Alyssa Royse is a writer, a speaker, and an educator who lives in Seattle with her husband and their menagerie of daughters and farm animals. Her work appears regularly on major sites all over the Web, often on televisions at conferences, and perpetually on her eponymous blog (www.alyssaroyse.com). Someday there will be awesome films and TV series made from her experiences, though right now they only exist in written form on her hard drive. If you know her, you will probably be in them, but really, every character is her.

talk to my lawyer

THE LEGALITIES OF WRITING ABOUT OTHERS

- -

"The names of the men in this book have been changed because most of them are named Dave."
—OPHIRA EISENBERG

- -

One out of every three students working on a memoir asks me: Can I get sued? Judith Barrington, in an appendix chapter about memoir and the law in *Writing the Memoir: From Truth to Art*, from which much of this chapter is drawn (in other words, buy her book to find out more!), says that when memoirists worry about being sued, it is "a way of focusing their fear of telling the truth." I love that interpretation, because it makes so much sense. The fact is that very few people are actually sued after writing memoirs. It does happen from time to time, of course. But those cases are often thrown out before they even make it to court due to some very real protections writers have on their side.

Barrington notes that there are two main reasons why you are very unlikely to be sued. One is that lawsuits are extremely expensive. Most people simply don't have the funds to pay a lawyer their often exorbitant fees. The second is that someone who pursues a lawsuit because he doesn't like your account of a situation will be advised by a lawyer that making a case will only further publicize the situation, even if the lawyer thinks that person has a case. Usually there is no case. Think about celebrities. Almost daily, lies are spread about them through publications like *Star* magazine. Millions of people read those rags! Celebrities don't usually waste their money on lawyers to try to get *Star* to recant what they wrote. Instead they trust that *Star*'s stories will not affect their careers in any real way. This is the case with your memoir as well. It is unlikely that what you write in a memoir will economically affect someone else's current life. It might affect them *emotionally*, but emotional damages are difficult to argue in court.

Likewise, people angry enough to sue are usually just that—angry. They will calm down after a while. We all do.

Finally, your publisher has experience with this issue. Most publishing houses, particularly the larger ones, have consulting lawyers who will give you and your editor the information you need. Jillian Lauren noted that her publisher's lawyer worked through the entire book, paragraph by paragraph, from a legal standpoint. By the time the book came out, she was confident that legally she was safe.

Then again, you still have to do your homework. There are two areas of law concerning memoir writing: defamation and invasion of privacy. Writersdigest.com notes the following.

> When you sign a publishing contract, you promise that
> your work will not defame anyone or invade anyone's
> privacy (along with a number of other assurances)—and

you agree to indemnify the publisher in the event of a lawsuit against your work. In other words, the onus is on you to deal with any legal troubles that come your way. Most self-publishing companies have similar clauses.[1]

In the passage below, Barrington assures writers that if they just use common sense, they will probably be all right.

The law reinforces what you already know as a responsible writer: You need to stick to the truth, and you need to be meticulous about your facts when someone else's reputation could be harmed.

FACT CHECKING

Memory is a terribly slippery subject. It resides mostly in the hippocampus, a small, seahorse-shaped section of the limbic system, and as such is not a *thing* at all. Memory is quite subjective, created through electrical impulses that travel through the brain. History is slippery as well, but in history books many people must corroborate events and facts. In memoirs, of course, we don't get such corroboration. Sometimes, the things that happened were witnessed by only you and one other person. Other times, they were experienced by the entire family but in different ways. Memoir is the story of memories—of *your* memories—and although you have a responsibility to not cause undue harm, you are also entitled to your own *experience* of the events.

In this way, memoir is tricky. It isn't journalism. It isn't a history textbook. It isn't even your autobiography. It is a story you remember that ties together a series of life events into an understandable, glittering package. But it is unlikely to be the same story as your sister's, your ex-wife's, or your friend's.

---

1 www.writersdigest.com/writing-articles/by-writing-goal/get-published-sell-my-work/defamation-and-invasion

When I wrote *Loose Girl*, I found out just how tricky fact checking can be. Because a rash of fiction books masquerading as memoir had been released at the time, my editor asked me to "prove" that the events in the book had actually happened. But how could I prove shameful, stolen moments with men whose names I could barely remember, who surely didn't remember me, and who I had no way of contacting anymore? I sent her copies of my diplomas from the places I got degrees from. Beyond that, there was little I could do.

Opinions and beliefs are protected by the First Amendment. There is a difference between saying someone *is* something and saying that you *believe* him to be something. The publisher's lawyer for the United Kingdom version of *Loose Girl* had me remove the line "He was bad," written about a "bad-boy" character, because I wasn't willing to change the voice to say, "I believed he was bad." In my mind, it would have destroyed the lyricism of the paragraph. In other words, I had to choose between the integrity of my voice and the possibility of legal consequences.

Another example came from a student in a memoir class. She aimed to portray her ex-husband, whom she claimed was a classic narcissist. Rather than ever use the word *narcissist*, I encouraged her to show her husband's behavior. Share what he said, how he moved through the room, what sorts of gestures he made, and so on. Good craft decisions can often save writers from putting themselves in legal harm's way.

How rigorous you are about your fact checking is partially up to you and partially up to your publisher. Kevin Sampsell, author of *A Common Pornography*, shared the following fact-checking experience.

> I had a brief phone meeting (maybe thirty minutes at the longest) with a HarperCollins lawyer. They seemed confident that the way I wrote the book was not going to cause any legal problems. When I published with *Salon*, I remember reading through some very seriously worded e-mails about fact checking and possible legal issues. It seems like journalistic websites and magazines are

being more cautious and discerning about what they're publishing these days, when it involves other people.

Robert C. Rummel-Hudson, author of *Schuyler's Monster,* had a markedly different experience with his publisher.

> I spent five hours on the phone with the attorney for St. Martin's, going over the book line by line. It was exhausting. Interestingly the things he wanted clarified or changed were never about avoiding pissing anyone off. Was it true? Was it clear? That was enough.

And finally, in the passage below, Victoria Loustalot, author of *This Is How You Say Goodbye,* discusses the fact-checking process.

> Obviously my editor and publishing house want the book to be factual, and to that end, they hire outside council to review every nonfiction book they publish. The key word there, though, is *review.* My book was not fact-checked by anyone other than myself. Publishers have neither the time nor the resources to do that. And my contract with my house is clear on this point. So, ultimately, if I get sued, I'm on my own. My publisher cannot be held responsible if it turns out my dad is alive and well and heterosexual and happily married to my mom.

INVASION OF PRIVACY

On his blog *The Rights of Writers,* attorney Mark Fowler weighs in on the other legal concern memoirists may potentially face: invasion of privacy. The disclosure of one's private life is actionable in many states. However, a plaintiff would have to prove the following.

> (1) publicity was given to matters concerning the plaintiff's private life;

(2) the matters made public would be highly offensive to
a reasonable person of ordinary sensibilities; and
(3) the matters publicized were not newsworthy, i.e., not
of legitimate public interest."[2]

This means that the facts must not already be a matter of public record
and the definition of what is offensive is based on community standards. This is why, when I described an ex-boyfriend using marijuana,
my publisher advised me to make sure that the ex wouldn't be angry. I
was quite sure he wouldn't be, but I was wrong. He didn't sue me, but
he let me know he felt violated and no longer wanted to be in contact.

Another way to invade privacy is to use facts in ways that mislead.
For instance, I described that aforementioned "bad boy" as dark and
unavailable, and I showed him ripping the library pocket from a book
about Jimi Hendrix. But I didn't show him patting a dog tied up outside the corner store. I didn't suggest that he had a mom and dad somewhere wondering when he would be home. I used the facts that could
be interpreted as "bad" in order to serve my book's purpose. It's easy
to see how this isn't fair to him.

The laws listed above are subject to a variety of "it all depends" sce-
narios. If the subject is a public figure, "public interest" can play a heavy
role. Susanna Kaysen, author of *Girl, Interrupted* and *The Camera My
Mother Gave Me,* was sued by an ex-boyfriend, Joseph Bonome, because she described him responding abusively when she was unwilling
to have sex. Because his potential abuse was "a matter of legitimate
public concern," the judge ruled in Kaysen's favor. Here is the description of the case, according to Mark Fowler.

> Although he was not named in the book, the boyfriend
> sued for invasion of privacy, arguing that many people
> knew that he had been Kaysen's companion and un-
> derstood that Kaysen was referring to him. The judge

---

2 www.rightsofwriters.com/2011/01/can-you-tell-your-own-true-story-even.html

dismissed the claim, finding that the disclosures were a matter of legitimate public concern. In the following passage, the judge explains his reasoning.

> In this case, it is critical that Kaysen was not a disinterested third party telling Bonome's personal story in order to develop the themes in her book. Rather, she is telling her own personal story—which inextricably involves Bonome in an intimate way ... it is within the context of Bonome and Kaysen's lives being inextricably bound together by their intimate relationship that the disclosures in this case must be viewed. Because the First Amendment protects Kaysen's ability to contribute her own personal experiences to the public discourse on important and legitimate issues of public concern, disclosing Bonome's involvement in those experiences is a necessary incident thereto.[3]

Augusten Burroughs was sued by the Turcotte family for his portrayal of them in *Running with Scissors: A Memoir*. According to the case, they sued for invasion of privacy, defamation (see the section on defamation in this chapter), and emotional damages, based on their claim that he outright lied about their family's behavior. Although Burroughs refers to them as "the Finches" in the book, the Turcottes noted that their privacy was invaded because their identities were obvious based on the book's description and because they were a notable family in Northampton, Massachusetts. Indeed there are actually directions to their house from the center of town in the book. In the end, the two parties reached an undisclosed settlement in which Burroughs admitted that the book was based only loosely on his life, making the book more fiction than memoir.

---

3 www.rightsofwriters.com/2011/01/can-you-tell-your-own-true-story-even.html

DEFAMATION

Defamation is a statement that is detrimental to a person's reputation. To be ruled defamatory, a statement must meet several criteria. First, it must be false, which lawyer and author Rachel Fehily explains here.

> The author must prove that the statement is based on an opinion and that opinion is honestly held. The writer must show that he or she believed in the truth of the opinion at the time of the publication of the statement, that the opinion is based on allegations of fact, and that the opinion related to matters of public interest.[4]

Additionally, the statement must be published, as consented by the plaintiff, and it must be stated as fact. Consider Robert C. Rummel-Hudson's experience writing about his neighbor with questionable proclivities.

> I actually had to make changes to a story about our next-door neighbors in Detroit, who watched porn on a huge television that was clearly visible in the window. The changes I had to make? I had to make it clear which apartment it was so that none of our other neighbors could be accused of being big-window porn sharers. The actual porny neighbors? No worries. It was a true story, and that was protection enough.

The statement must also be about a named or identifiable person. This is where it might be wise to change names and identifying details. Remember the ex-boyfriend who was angry that I said he smoked pot? Well, he was also angry that, even though I changed his name, I noted the state he was from, where he went to college (because we went together), and where we moved together afterward. He told me that everyone knew he was "Leif," whether they knew me or not.

---

4 www.writing.ie/resources/defamation-staying-out-of-trouble-when-writing-non-fiction-with-rachel-fehily

The statement must be about a living person; no one can sue on behalf of a dead person. And, finally, the statement must be damaging and injurious to the person concerned. This means that the person must be held in public contempt or that the statement damages finances or relationships. The Turcotte family in Burroughs's story was particularly incensed about the way they were portrayed.

> Events in the book which the suit claims are false include the Turcottes' condoning sexual affairs between children and adults, Turcotte's wife eating dog food, and the family using an electroshock machine it stored under the stairs. The lawsuit claims the book also falsely portrays a home in unbelievable squalor, with a young child running around naked and defecating and old turkey being stored in the showers.[5]

One can see how these details might be damaging to the family's reputation and ability to find jobs or spouses.

Keep in mind, too, that corporations and religious groups can sue for defamation as well. Public figures have to prove that you wrote about them with "actual malice," meaning you knew what you wrote was not true or didn't care whether it was. People who aren't famous or in the public eye are not required to provide such proof.

HOW TO WRITE A MEMOIR WITHOUT GETTING SUED

As noted earlier, it's highly unlikely anyone will bring a successful lawsuit against you. However, there are certainly ethical approaches you can take to writing your memoir that will help reduce the already small likelihood of it happening.

---

5 web.archive.org/web/20061110081231/http://www.gazettenet.com/newsroom/in
dex.cfm/2006/10/18/Family-suing-Running-with-Scissors-author-settles-with-Sony

CHANGE NAMES AND HIDE IDENTIFYING DETAILS

Some students of memoir have thought that simply changing names makes a story fiction, but that's not the case at all. When you write memoir you *should* change names. You *should* change where that person works and what he or she looks like, unless those details are essential to the story. Likewise you can make a few people composites of each other. You can crunch time. You can say you were in Houston on that trip instead of Dallas. None of these things will stop your memoir from being a memoir. Hope Edelman shares her approach below.

> When I wrote *Motherless Daughters* in 1992–1993, no one asked me to provide backup materials to prove any of my claims. The publisher didn't even check to see if my mother had actually died from breast cancer when I was seventeen. But by the time I published *The Possibility of Everything* in 2009, the atmosphere surrounding memoir had changed considerably. Several books had been in the news for having fabricated material or even entire life stories, and several high-profile lawsuits had occurred. Publishing houses seemed to have become more wary as a result. Ballantine sent a questionnaire asking me to list all of the characters in the book and to specify when I'd used real names and when I'd used pseudonyms. They also wanted to know which characters, if any, were composites. I had already gone down to Belize to ask the people who appeared in the memoir for permission to use their real names and had secured it either in writing or on video in the cases where individuals weren't literate. I changed the names and identifying details of characters I couldn't track down, and the publisher seemed satisfied with that.

TELL THE TRUTH

What *does* make a memoir a memoir, then? Memoir happens when, even if you change names and details, even when you crunch time, the things that happened *actually happened*. James Frey got lambasted because the things in his book didn't happen to him. He was only in jail very briefly. He didn't do many of the things he claimed to have done in the memoir. In a note to his readers, he said, "People cope with adversity in many different ways, ways that are deeply personal. ... My mistake ... is writing about the person I created in my mind to help me cope and not the person who went through the experience." Frey lost track of what makes memoir a true story. The person you wish you were—that's the stuff of fiction. The one who stumbled through adversity, the one who really was there, who did shameful things, who failed to be cool or shocking or strong—that's memoir. Tell the truth. Tell the real truth.

GET CONSENT FROM THE PEOPLE YOU WRITE ABOUT

Obviously you can't get consent from everyone you include in your memoir. But you can get approval from some. Because my sister was a major character in *Loose Girl*, I sent her the manuscript before it went to copyediting. She didn't agree entirely with my portrayal of her, but she understood that this was my memoir, my memories and experience, not hers. Many of the writers quoted in this book chose to share their memoirs or parts of their memoirs with people in their books. As we've noted in past chapters, this is a tricky process. You don't want to set yourself up to be told, "If you publish this, I'll ruin you," or to have someone tell you, "Your memory is wrong. I didn't do that at all." Pick readers carefully. Protect your work's integrity. Also, give your readers fair warning. Make clear what you will or won't change. Define memoir as the story of *your* memories. Note that while you hope they will feel respected by you letting them read the book, you also hope they will respect you by understanding that this is your story, one you needed to write through to understand.

EXERCISES

1. Review scenes in your memoir that expose something undesirable about someone. Is this exposure necessary to your narrative? If so, does it clearly identify the person as the character in your memoir? Is there another way to illustrate this aspect of the character without either exposing this detail or fictionalizing an event? If so, how might you illustrate this aspect by rewriting the existing scene or writing a new scene?

2. Make a list of the names and identifying traits of the characters in your memoir. What details could you change to protect yourself as an author and the people in your memoir? With those details in mind, make a second list with the names and identifying characteristics changed.

3. As discussed in this chapter, publishers often expect authors to do their own fact checking. Make a list of factual details such as names and dates that you need to check before submitting your memoir to a publisher. Remember, memory by its very nature is subjective, and even seemingly unimportant inaccuracies can be important to the protection, credibility, and reception of your memoir.

4. Issues such as invasion of privacy and defamation don't always have clear legal parameters. For example, an invasion of privacy might mean publicizing the private life of someone who isn't of legitimate public interest in a way that is highly offensive to a person of ordinary sensibilities. Similarly, defamation or misrepresentation is typically understood

as a consciously inaccurate statement that is detrimental to a person's reputation in the eyes of general society and irrelevant to matters of public interest. Given these loose parameters, identify parts of your memoir that could provoke litigation, and contact legal counsel for advice about how to protect yourself as an author and those in your memoir.

DEPARTNERED:
THE FORGOTTEN MEMOIR
Vincent Truman

This is a memoir about a memoir.

November 2011: Immediately following a glorious three-day road trip from Las Cruces, New Mexico, to Chicago, Illinois, to transport home my childhood bedroom set that my mother had graciously held for me for a third of a century, the wife let me know that she wanted a separation. Possibly even a divorce. While I was aware we had a few problems (see Every Other Couple in the World), I had no idea this was coming. A reply was warranted, certainly, but I admit I had no idea what that reply might look like. I did not wish to say, "Yes," as that would bring our marriage to a rather unceremonious end. I did not wish to say, "No," as that might appear argumentative, and the last thing I wanted was for the wife to retort, "See: We can't even agree on getting a separation! The only recourse then is to, of course, separate!" So I said the first thing that came to mind: "If we do that, I'll burn the house down."

Now, I had no intention of burning the house down. Even more than that, I lacked the skill set to burn down a house and hide the cause from insurance adjusters. However, I simply wanted to say something that might decelerate, dissuade, or distract the wife from this wish that had completely taken me by surprise. I immediately regretted saying it, though, as it was hurled at me frequently in the subsequent months. "You said you'd burn the house down," the wife would snarl. "How can I trust you?" The epilogue to our marriage was being written, no matter what I said, did, threatened, implied, begged, intimated, or groaned. My partner was leaving, and there was little I could do about it.

Divorce is the adult version of cooties. Most people who hear about it tend to move to the other end of the playground posthaste. Allegiances and alliances form overnight and not always along party lines. The cruelest irony was, of course, that the one person who I would share my most intimate and honest feelings with just happened to be the person who wanted nothing to do with me. Feeling like a character viciously yanked out of a Harlequin Romance and dumped into a Stephen King novel (with snow), I retreated to my office to begin writing a diary, hoping that translating thoughts and feelings into words would, in some way, shed some light on exactly why this was happening. (No reason from the wife was given, nor did it ever come.) This diary would in time become a 230-page memoir titled *Departnered: A Virtual Memoir of Marriage, Divorce and Pixels*.

A side note over the odd name of my book: One of the key ingredients in the dissolution of my marriage, to say nothing of the civility between the wife and me, was the virtual online game *Second Life*. In *Second Life*, a player can create representations, or avatars, of himself and hop around in a 3-D world, seeking out whatever piques one's interest. Both the wife and I played the game in the early days of our courtship—prior to cohabitating, we would have "geek dates" in which our SL avatars would go to virtual clubs and click on blue and pink balls, which would manipulate our avatars into dancing with each other—but by 2011, when we could have invested time in our marriage, our home, and our two cats, we tended to hang out in our own *Second Life* cliques. The wife found like-minded people who specialized in high school double entendre and Duran Duran music. I had created a female avatar and had become fascinated by experiencing firsthand not only how men lavished attention on women (something that, as a man, rarely if ever happened to me) but also how lousy they were at it. By November 2011, I had grown bored with *Second Life*, but the wife had grown more interested in building a virtual island with three other friends, which they dubbed Unfourgettable (get it?), and listening to the latest remixes of "Hungry Like the Wolf." In *Second Life*, as in real life, we remained married (or "partnered" as they call it in the game).

And then came the day the wife said, "If I go, I betray you. If I stay, I betray me." To this day, I'm not sure what she meant by that—it sounded like a script written by committee—but it definitely signaled the end of our partnership.

The separation began in January 2012 when the wife moved out; it wasn't long before she departnered me on *Second Life*. Two months later, she said she wanted to divorce. Still feeling like a dutiful husband, I volunteered to handle all of the paperwork and legwork, including going to court. In May 2012, I found myself before a judge in Chicago's Daley Center, representing the wife and me, to request the marriage be dissolved. I still didn't want the divorce, but, as the saying goes, it takes two to tangle. Wearing the same black suit I wore on my wedding day, I took a series of pictures in front of the Picasso in Daley Plaza, just like the wife and I had done the morning we were married in August 2009. This time, though, I was alone.

By this time, the wife had ceased communicating with me altogether. Although she knew I was handling the divorce (she signed the affidavit permitting me to represent us both), she made no inquiry as to its status, then or ever.

During the months of January through October 2012, the only peace I found was when I sat to write in my diary. I wrote about being unable to kiss the first girlfriend I had after the divorce because part of me saw her as "another woman"—so used to marriage as I was. I described the Month of Crying, during which every night was not complete until I wound up on the floor in a fetal position, terrified yet curiously marveling at the wounded-animal yelps that would escape my mouth. I assayed the Museum of Missing Pieces, the nickname I gave to our home after 50 percent of the furniture was removed, which resembled nothing so much as a high-concept art exhibit about half-life. I inventoried any and all flaws that were either gifted to or created by me. I longed for a physical tombstone I could visit for the death of my marriage, which felt no less devastating than the sudden demise of a best friend. (Eventually I did visit my ex-wife's father's gravestone in Arlington National Cemetery, and it was there I left my wedding ring.)

Finally, two hundred pages and two hundred days later, I was ready for something other than mourning. I was never told the reason why the marriage failed or why the wife was so unhappy, but I realized waiting for the reason would be hanging on to something that didn't exist anymore. I consciously chose to forgive and reintroduced myself to the idea that I will always love my ex-wife and that love wanted only for her to find peace in her own way.

The writing slowed and ceased; I had reached a natural break. Bolstered by a new group of friends and my divorce support group (now dubbed "Divorce Camp"), I decided my last step in self-healing would be to self-publish *Departnered* as a rocky road map for those going through something similar. On November 7, 2012, almost on the anniversary of the separation itself, I put the book out. A week later, I was sued.

The ex-wife, in her complaint, did not dispute any of the text; there were no claims of libel or slander. Her issues boiled down to one poor reason and one understandable one. The poor one: She claimed, since I had started the book when we were still married, it was a marital asset and she deserved half of the proceeds. The understandable one: She really, really, really didn't like the cover. The claim went on to suggest that, because I had misrepresented my marital assets, the divorce itself should be dissolved.

The cover of *Departnered* depicted me in my black suit, taken on the day of the divorce hearing, standing in the same place I had stood with my wife on our wedding day. Instead of the wife, though, I had edited into the picture a representation of her avatar from *Second Life* wearing a low-cut V-neck dress, her eyes slightly crossed, attending a virtual bachelorette party and holding a virtual penis sucker in her hand.

The claim, made on the ex-wife's behalf by an intellectual-property firm, of all things, implied that I had stolen her likeness. In fact, I had stolen a likeness she had purchased in a virtual video game, which was owned by *Second Life*'s company, Linden Lab. If nothing else, her claim illustrated just how much she identified with her *Second Life* persona.

I contacted an attorney friend of mine from Divorce Camp for advice and representation. He indicated she had little to no case and suggested I fight it. In the worst-case scenario, he opined, we'd wind up married again and I might have the opportunity to go after her assets (specifically, a new condo that she had purchased after the divorce but that would become a marital asset if we found ourselves married again). It sounded like a good counterclaim, but because I could sense that what she really didn't like was having her avatar on and in my book, I told my attorney to just settle. Fighting her through attorneys seemed ridiculous, especially considering we handled the divorce wholly on our own, and being married to her again seemed even more absurd.

After about a month, the settlement was arrived at. I was not to use her avatar in any publication. I was not to publish or promote *Departnered* for any commercial purpose. And, at the end, there was an added strange bonus: I apparently had in my possession, according to the ex-wife, compromising pictures of her. Some nude and some seminude. I was to destroy and delete any and all copies of the pictures; otherwise the settlement would not go through. I called my lawyer. "I don't know what this last thingy is about," I said, showing off my lack of legalese. "I don't have any nude or seminude pictures of my ex-wife."

He said, "That's fine if you don't. She wants it in there. She wants it in a public document that she took nudes somewhere and thinks they're with you. So, fuck her. Just make sure you don't have any, anywhere."

"Yeah, all right. If this goes away today because I sign it, that's fine with me."

So I signed, the Agreed Order was entered, and I pulled *Departnered* from any commercial publication.

My lawyer friend later told me, "You know what you could do? You could write the book from scratch again today, and she'd have no grounds whatsoever to sue. And since those *Second Life* avatars all look the same, pick another one and put it in your ex-wife's place."

I considered that option for about two-and-a-half minutes. But my peace was made. I forgave the ex-wife. I loved the ex-wife and wanted her to be happy—and a book by me about our Kardashian-style marriage and divorce wouldn't help either one of us get happier. So instead I ordered a few copies of the book for my own collection and deleted the master files. Our story was over.

Vincent Truman is a playwright, an author, and a performer in Chicago. As a playwright, he has written ten plays, including the gender-bending *Venus Envy* and *The Observatory*, which was ranked one of the top twenty independent-theater pieces of 2010. He has written two books: the short-story compilation *Ugly Bungalow* and a collection of comic illustrations titled *This Is My First Time So Please Be Brutal and Other Cartoons*. Additionally he was the founder of a compilation series titled *Uno Kudo* and is a bit of a storyteller, making the rounds at reading series hosted by The Moth, Do Not Submit, Pungent Parlor, *The Logan Square Literary Review*, and others. He is divorced and owns a cat.

AN UNEXPECTED RESPONSE
Ellen Currey-Wilson

I grew up in a family of what could easily be called a colorful cast of characters. I often thought we should all be in a book, but I didn't consider writing that book until I became a parent. As a new mother, I was obsessed with the role that television played in the lives of families, since I had been hooked on the plug-in drug most of my life. I knew I had to write about it.

My memoir is called *The Big Turnoff: Confessions of a TV-Addicted Mom Trying to Raise a TV-Free Kid* and was published by Algonquin in 2007. It chronicles the first eight years of my son's life and my attempt to kick my television habit. The pages are filled with background from my childhood, including some unflattering but often entertaining portrayals of my eccentric mother and siblings.

Writing served as a fabulous escape for me and an excellent television replacement. My book took on a life all its own. I forced myself not to think about how my family and friends might react when they eventually found themselves on the pages of a memoir. To consider their feelings while I was writing would have halted my creative flow. Instead I liked to imagine that everyone would be magically overjoyed after reading my book. I've always been good at deluding myself.

It was only after my publisher set the date for my book's release that I began to worry. I decided I should at least prepare those closest to me, rather than surprise them. I started with my husband, handing him my newly edited manuscript and making a confession.

"I've written about our sex life," I said. "Just a little bit."

He looked wary, probably because a week earlier I had told him I had done *just a little bit* of shopping, when I'd actually ordered new living room furniture.

"The sex parts are really funny," I reassured him.

He looked irritated. I guess he didn't think our sex life was a laughing matter.

"It was out of my hands," I explained. "I was at the service of the art itself. That's what dictated what had to be in the book."

"Whatever," he said, looking unconvinced.

Fortunately, when he read the manuscript, he didn't recommend changing anything. His siblings, on the other hand, reacted squeamishly when he told them about the sex scenes.

"I don't want to read what my brother does in the bedroom," his older sister insisted.

I wondered with growing apprehension how my own siblings would react. I gave my brother the manuscript shortly before it went to press.

"You should have consulted me sooner," he complained after reading it. "I was manufacturing high-quality meth, and you made it sound like I was an amateur! I would have explained the difference to you if you'd asked me sooner."

I considered giving the manuscript to my sister, too, but in the end I simply couldn't do it. If I had to change something she didn't like, I was sure my story would be compromised. I hadn't revealed any of her deep, dark secrets. I'd simply written about the things she had shared with me and those in her hippie community. I talked about her admiration of breatharians, for example: people who live in Nepal and have subsisted on air alone.

"Don't you think you should at least prepare her before the book comes out?" my husband warned.

In the end I showed up at her house a few days before the book's release and apologized for what she would soon be reading. In an attempt to alleviate my guilt, I impulsively offered her my portion of the inheritance our recently departed mother had left us, an impulse I regret to this day far more than anything I've ever written about anyone.

Aside from family, I only let three other people read the manuscript ahead of time, and they were my closest friends. As I had portrayed all of them in a positive light, I was not surprised when they told me they were pleased. Sadly, I didn't show the manuscript to my friend Bernice (not her real name) because I knew she would be unhappy with it. I decided to at least forewarn her, which went poorly.

"You wrote about my affair, didn't you?" she accused me.

I tried to reassure her that no one reading the book would realize I was writing about her situation.

"I gave the guy you were seeing a different occupation," I said. "I made him an actor, for God's sake!"

I then told her about the disclaimer at the beginning of the book, but she didn't care. I later discovered, much to my disappointment, that most people didn't bother to read the disclaimer. Admittedly it was a mouthful.

> To protect the privacy of people mentioned in this book, characters have been combined and situations disguised, and certain names, places and other identifying characteristics have been changed.

In other words, I had license to write pretty much anything. Maybe that's why there were folks who thought I had written about them, when in fact I had not.

Even so, I had written about lots of people. I hadn't realized just how many until the book came out. Everywhere I went, from the grocery store to the cleaners, I ran into my characters, often taking time to chat with them, all the while hoping my relationship with these people wouldn't change, that they would never find out about the book, much less read it. I had no idea I would feel so exposed.

I remember taking my son, Casey, to school shortly after the book's release, dropping him off at the curb. Usually I would park my car afterward and then join some of my friends to go for a run or have coffee together. I've always loved my son's school, and for the most part my memoir reflects this. I had written about Casey's teachers in glowing terms, that is, except for his kindergarten teacher. I wondered if I would ever feel comfortable there again.

I drove to the Starbucks far away from Casey's school and even farther away from my neighborhood and the people I had written about there.

"Where were you?" my friend Isabel asked the next day.

"I had to be somewhere else," I said evasively, not wanting to tell her I was afraid of running into the kindergarten teacher.

In truth I was also busy. The first few weeks around the book's release, I was doing radio interviews with NPR-affiliate stations on the other side of the country and later appearing on television in England. I found it easy to talk about the "electronic babysitter" with people I didn't know and would probably never meet again. I spoke about shows that targeted infants even though the American Academy of Pediatrics didn't recommend any television for children under two. I shared my personal experiences with television addiction and the challenges I faced raising my own child. I talked about how difficult it is for parents everywhere to raise kids without a strong support system and sufficient resources.

I wanted people to read my book. I just didn't want anyone in Portland—or anyone I knew for that matter—to read it. I didn't send group e-mails or post announcements on Facebook about my upcoming interviews and events. When I ran into people in town who had heard about the book, I discouraged them from buying it.

"Please don't read it," I would say. "I don't think it's your type of book."

These are not the words a publisher wants to hear. What's worse is I didn't like saying the name of the book.

"It's not a very good title," I would tell people who asked about it.

I wanted to keep my life a secret. I worried about my son, too, and the effect my book might have on him. I had disclosed intimate details of his life, of our lives together. I was pretty sure at some point he wouldn't appreciate having others find out that his kindergarten teacher thought he was odd.

Fortunately Casey had yet to read my book. He was only eleven when it came out, and the sex scenes alone made the book inappropriate for anyone under thirteen. But some of the parents of his friends had read it, and most had heard about it. I could tell by the way they acted around me.

"Can your son watch television at our house?" they would ask me anxiously.

"Sure," I would say.

I wanted to tell them that if they had read my book, they would know that by the end I was no longer a zealot, just another parent trying to do her best and often falling short. I didn't like drawing unnecessary attention to my child or making other parents feel uncomfortable, or worse, inadequate.

In writing this book, I had made the decision to tell the world about my son, but paradoxically I now wanted above all to protect him. I worried that he would feel pressured to become a poster boy for TV-free living. He would think he had to live up to the ideals I had written about, always remaining smart and focused, creative and fit. These expectations could become a burden, one he shouldn't have to carry. In addition, I had to keep my own ego in check so he could live his life the way he wanted, not necessarily the way I thought it should be.

Fortunately, after some time passed, I began to relax. I became comfortable for the most part with my friends and in my community. My friend Bernice remained angry and hurt, not only because I had written about her affair but also because I hadn't shown the manuscript to her ahead of time.

"You let your other friends read it before it came out!" she hissed. "You chose them over me!"

I thought long and hard about what she said and knew it was true. There were relationships I had been willing to sacrifice for the sake of my story. I had carefully chosen those I would be willing to throw under the bus, per se, in spite of my love for them, because I wanted to deliver my message in the most effective way possible. I had betrayed the trust of my sister because of her entertainment value. Maybe I had betrayed myself, too, portraying my own character in a less than favorable light at times. But I spared my husband, keeping what's sacred between us, thereby holding on to the marriage. That was a choice, too.

As time passed most everyone in the book forgave me, and I've forgiven everyone, too, including myself. Even so, my friends still pause midsentence sometimes and glare at me.

"You better not write about this," they warn me. "What I'm telling you is personal."

"Don't worry," I reassure them.

My son doesn't say this anymore. He's forgiven me, too, and he's not a bad writer himself. He's already written an essay about me, and I have to admit it wasn't easy for me to read.

"It's supposed to be funny," he said.

"Sure," I said. "I guess it is."

Writing about others can be messy at times, so I'm thankful for those writers who are brave enough to do it, to share their feelings, which so often mirror my own. I love memoirs, but I don't intend to write another one.

My new book is a novel, and I can hardly wait to find the right publisher. Most of all I'm looking forward to being interviewed about it. I can hear the questions now.

"Are any of your characters based on people you know?" the reporter will ask.

"It's a work of fiction," I will answer. "The characters spring from my imagination." Then I will smile. "I have a great imagination."

Ellen Currey-Wilson is the author of the memoir *The Big Turnoff: Confessions of a TV-Addicted Mom Trying to Raise a TV-Free Kid*, published in 2007 by Algonquin Books in the United States and Fusion Press in the United Kingdom. She's written numerous articles and has been featured in a variety of radio programs, newspapers, and magazines in the United States and England. Ellen lives in Portland with her husband and occasionally their son, who is a sophomore at UC Berkeley. Her new novel, *Leaving Texas*, is awaiting representation.

CHAPTER EIGHT

expect the unexpected

THE MEDIA'S RESPONSE TO YOUR MEMOIR

"I am not afraid to be hated/I am not afraid to be loved ..."

—JOY HARJO, "I GIVE IT BACK: A POEM TO GET RID OF FEAR"

Before the Internet, writers wrote essays and articles that were not immediately accessible to millions of viewers. Neither did readers have the opportunity to express their knee-jerk reactions to writers about their work. Readers sent letters to agents, who then sent those on to the authors. Whether those letters were fan mail or hate mail, they took thought and time to send and write. But now, most writers I know have a story to tell about the "takedown culture" in which we live.

Lynn Beisner discusses the reactions and criticism she received after writing her controversial essay "I Wish My Mother Had Aborted Me."

> I have had people diagnose me with various mental illnesses that I am fortunate not to have. People have said that I write out of revenge against my mother, which I do not. At least one critic went through all of my Twitter feed, my public Facebook profile, and my entire body of work online and deduced from it that I am lying about having been physically abused as a child. Another person used observations from the in-depth research on me to come to a different conclusion: that I was writing simply to make Christianity look bad.

Abby Mims says the following about the reaction she received to her essay "Joshua Ferris Is My Nemesis."

> This was a hard, strange lesson I learned last year after writing about my "nemesis" in graduate school, who has gone on to become wildly acclaimed in the literary world. … It was meant to be a generally funny piece, poking fun at my own naiveté and bad behavior ten years ago and the ways in which I've moved forward since. I thought it would be interesting to reflect on the experience a decade later and to see for myself how I felt about things. I felt better about the experience, like I had finally exorcised it after I wrote it, but publishing it was a whole different ballgame. People picked sides and either declared me a crazy, jealous bitch or vehemently defended me and related entirely. The bonus was getting amazing e-mails from strangers about how much they loved the honesty of the piece and connecting with

several incredible women writers about it, as some of
the theme was about the boys' club of academia.

The jolting and disturbing downside was having
strangers attack my character [and] my motives and/
or declaring that I simply wasn't as hard a worker or as
talented as he was, which is why I hadn't succeeded as
a writer. Perhaps the most disturbing development was
a series of very angry e-mails from a professor I mentioned in the essay, calling me pathetic [and] a coward
and declaring himself my enemy.

I have a story as well. My first takedown was after an interview with
Marie Claire about *Loose Girl*, which was scheduled for release the
following month. Someone at a news site got wind of it and wrote a
scathing article about me. More than 265 commenters joined in. Two
additional well-known writers picked up on *that* article and joined in
the fury. The book hadn't even come out yet!

To say I was devastated is an understatement. I was terrified of
what was to come. The dread and anger at being misunderstood
by strangers who hadn't read my book yet (and probably now never
would) ate me up at night, keeping me awake. I remembered that my
agent had warned me when I'd sent in the manuscript. He said, "Are
you sure you want to do this? It's sensitive material. People might get
upset. They might hurt you." I'd brushed off his warning. I'd read
plenty of memoirs with sensitive subject matter. They'd all freed me.
I'd appreciated their honesty and raw exploration of difficult material. I couldn't fathom that anyone else would have responded another
way. Boy, was I wrong.

Lynn Beisner adds, "Be prepared for fifteen minutes of fame. I
know that you think that you would just be grateful for it and would
bask in it. But it is far more stressful than you can even imagine." Many
newer writers, like I was, like Beisner was, don't consider anything but
our intentions—always good!—when we put something out into the

world. When you write about other people, you have an ethical responsibility to treat them as fairly as possible and to protect their privacy as much as possible. But are you responsible for the ways in which complete strangers will respond?

Gone is the age in which *The New York Times Book Review* is the primary source of opinions about books. Now anyone can have an Amazon or Goodreads account and announce what they think of your writing to anyone who will listen. They can trash your character rather than your writing. Now bloggers get to say what they want about your work, and your great uncle's opinion carries as much weight in a comment thread on an article in *The Nation* as a professor emeritus of economics at Harvard. Obviously this is also good news. It's easier to get your work published online than it used to be, because there are so many outlets to do so. Also, you could start your own blog, market it well, and wind up with a book deal someday. But, with less vetting of writers and critics, freelance-writing and book-critic jobs are mostly defunct. Becoming a writer used to mean many years of apprenticeship and study under those who had worked hard to get published. Those days are quickly disappearing.

Much more concerning is how often hateful speech, cyberbullying, and character assassination has taken the place of thoughtful discourse. At this point, comment sections are so full of vitriol, snark, and personal attacks that they're rarely worth reading.

So that's the bad news. The good news is that the readers who identify with your work and who are saved, who are grateful and moved by it, will let you know as well. They will send you e-mails and private Facebook messages, and they'll mention you on Twitter. They will write Amazon reviews as well. And they wouldn't be able to do that without the advent of social media and the Internet. So, to go back to the question of your responsibility to strangers, the answer is *no* and also *yes*. All you can do is write your story with as much integrity and honesty as you can and care for the people you write about. That's it. The rest is out of your control.

WHAT TO EXPECT FROM THE MEDIA'S REACTIONS

The point of this chapter is to clarify that you *can't* know how the media will respond to your memoir. However, you can be as prepared as possible by considering how they might respond. Before *Loose Girl* was published, I was sure I'd get lambasted for writing a book about being a "slut." I wasn't prepared for the much bigger criticism I received, which was that I wasn't slut enough to write the book. I was blindsided. Here are some considerations to help you avoid the same experience.

- Your intentions might be misunderstood. In fact, you will probably be attacked by at least one reviewer or commenter. Lynn Beisner's account below reminds memoirists to expect the unexpected.

  Something that I was not ready for is that in many cases, people will not be angry at you for your story but rather for how you made sense of your story. For example: I was deeply distressed when I wrote about an incident of sexual assault. I expected some crazy people to tell me how I brought it on myself or [to] challenge some part of my narrative. Instead I was attacked because I had not framed my experience the way anti-rape activists wanted me to. It was incredibly disorienting.

- People might surprise you by responding most to a section of the book that means less to you than other parts. Or they might react to an essay or blog you threw together, one that, in your mind, is not as good as other pieces you wrote.
- The media is interested in sensationalism. Don't be surprised if in an interview the reporter brings up the most shocking or challenging parts of your book. Prepare answers.

- Never assume people won't read what you write and post it on the Internet for all to find.

Luckily there are some things you can do to prepare for the onslaught of attention. You can warn people you know that your essay has been posted. You can apply privacy settings to your own blog. You can pick and choose where you allow your work to be posted; i.e., Jezebel.com is famous for its readers' snarky comments. Also, as with the story I shared in the Introduction about the woman who wrote about her affair and subsequently wound up divorced, consider whether your message and your readers are worth what your writing will cost you.

HOW TO PREPARE FOR THE MEDIA'S REACTIONS

Now that you know what to potentially expect from the media, what can you do to prepare? Here are some tips.

- Don't read the comments. This is a hard one. Buried among the mean, hurtful comments often is kindness and support. All of us want to know what people think of our writing. All of us want kudos and accolades. One might argue, too, that it's good to hear criticism you might need. Still, *don't read the comments*. The ones that are there to simply get in a jab, to attack your character, will sink beneath your skin and stay. Dani Shapiro takes this tact as well.

  I didn't [read the comments]. Not because I wasn't interested. Not because I didn't care. But because I knew that there would be bruising, painful comments and that reading them would be like falling down a rabbit hole. The toxic comments—amidst all the others—would stick to my bones, while the supportive comments would wash over me like water. Like most of us, I am all-too-ready to think the worst of my-self. To censor myself. This soft underbelly is the place from which I write, and I must at all costs protect it.

If you do read the comments, however, have a plan in place for how you will respond or if you will respond at all. It's hard not to feel defensive when people attack and misunderstand you, but usually the best course of action is to stay silent. It's un-likely that people who are already angry or cruel enough to take the time to lampoon you on the In-ternet will hear your argument and come around to your side. Let it go. You can't control them or their feelings about you and your work.[1]

- Decide how you will handle press. Will you do interviews with everyone or only with those you believe understand your story? Consider the controversial nature of your work. Some news out-lets and online magazines have a clear political or social bent that you'll need to take into account. Others might only want to make fun of you (think Howard Stern). Maybe you're up for that, but it is good to decide ahead of time.

- If you do get misunderstood in a radio or television interview, have a graceful answer at the ready. I like to think about how we teach children to handle bullies. We tell them to respond in a way that makes clear to the bully that she has no control over him. We also tell them to stand up for the rights and in-tegrity of other children getting bullied. I try to incorporate both those ideas into my work as a writer. I brush off bullies and champion the victims.

- Remember that people are often overwhelmed with their own hurts and frustrations, and unfortunately we live in a culture of projection. Consider celebrities and all the gossip rags. We

---

1 danishapiro.com/on-living-out-loud

love to insult people whom we don't really know. We love to have opinions about people whose lives don't affect ours. Remember, too, that the anonymity of the Internet makes it even easier for people to express those opinions. Louis C.K. tells a joke about how we would never say to people's faces the things we do when we're protected behind the steel bodies of our cars. He says to imagine standing next to someone in an elevator who accidentally bumps into you. You wouldn't turn to him and say, "I hope you die!"

- Keep your fans in the foreground. Every single message you get from someone who was saved by your story or who identified with your work will ground you. They are the ones who will remind you why you write. There is nothing more gratifying than those notes. Savor them. Send back notes of gratitude. Print them out, and hang them on your wall. You earned them, and it's important to remember them during the bad times.

EXERCISES

1. Make a plan for dealing with the public's response to your memoir. Will you read what is written about your work? Will you have someone screen the comments, or will you read them yourself? Will you respond to criticism? How will you handle on-screen or radio interviews? What if your family and friends are contacted about your memoir? Consider your preferences and what steps you can take to prepare yourself and those around you for your memoir's publication.

2. Review your memoir for scenes or themes that might be considered controversial. Though authors can never pinpoint exactly what readers might find controversial,

consider how you might respond to criticism or questions regarding these issues. What is important for readers and the general public to know?

3. Consider how the publication of your memoir might affect certain aspects of your immediate life, such as your job and your social circles. Would your employer have a problem with your memoir? Could you discuss with them beforehand that you're planning to publish it? If so, what would be the best way for you to address the issue?

4. One of the hardest things authors face when they put their writing out into the world is keeping it protected from the outpouring of public commentary in the digital age. What precautions could you make to ensure the safety and authenticity of your writing? Consider things like making your social media profiles private or creating a separate page for all writing-related posts.

BAD BOY MEMOIR: WHEN ABUSERS TELL THEIR STORIES

Hugo Schwyzer

"If it happened to you, it's your story to tell."

As a blogger and contributing writer for several national outlets, I'd been a fierce and very public defender of this maxim. In a variety of short autobiographical pieces published on various websites, I shared often-graphic anecdotes from my own life story. Other people—ex-wives, girlfriends, old roommates—were always involved, and though I changed their names or otherwise obscured their identities, it was not impossible for a persistent reader to figure out who these other people were. When challenged, I argued for the almost unlimited right of the memoirist to tell the truth about what happened. I paraphrased Anne Lamott's quote that if people don't want you to write unkind things about them, they ought to have been nicer to you.

That stance, I have come to see, is both limited and cruel.

My fascination with brutal honesty was rooted in rebellion against a family ethos of smoothing over unpleasant truths. "Not all lies are bad," my mother told me when I was little, trying to teach me to be kinder by being less forthcoming. Having often been punished for fibbing, I was more than a little confused by Mom's typology of truth.

I remember when I was about eight, my younger brother and I were taken to visit an elderly relative for lunch. Mom knew just how bad this woman's cooking was likely to be, so she prepared us well. "You may not like the food. But you will eat all of it, and you will smile and not complain. You will say how delicious it was." Pip and I were promised Jack in the Box for dinner if we performed as expected. The lunch was worse than could be imagined: cold fish with limp salad greens and cottage cheese. It was a child's nightmare. Pip refused to eat it, but I devoured every morsel with feigned but restrained relish, knowing I'd be called out if I oversold the enthusiasm. *Think of the cheeseburger*, I told myself. It worked.

The aged cousin was happy; Mom was thrilled. On the way home, she praised me for doing what she knew had been difficult. "You see," she explained, "some lies make people feel good when honesty would only hurt their feelings. Part of growing up is knowing when you must tell the truth and when it's better to tell a kind white lie." That lesson was soon helpfully enforced with the fast food I loved so much.

Years later, I learned a more sophisticated aspect of the family art of dissembling for the sake of harmony. When I was a seventeen-year-old high school senior, I brought my first serious girlfriend, Marnie, for an Easter weekend at my family's Northern California ranch. Before we left, my mother pulled me aside to explain the rules. We needed to put our luggage in separate rooms, but discreet nocturnal traffic would be both permitted and ignored. The point was unmistakable: What matters isn't what you do but what other people see you doing. Pay public homage to propriety, and your private life—as long as it stays genuinely private—is entirely yours to enjoy as you see fit.

In my family, the Suitcase Rule remains very much in effect. It doesn't just govern where unmarried couples sleep. It covers how we speak about almost every aspect of our lives. This doesn't mean that there's no space for talking about uncomfortable truths—just no space for talking about them outside a closed family circle (or a therapist's office). "You can do whatever you like as long as you don't do it in the streets and frighten the horses." More than one family member likes to paraphrase that Oscar Wilde maxim to explain our collective emphasis on private latitude coupled with stringent public discretion.

By the time I was old enough to learn the Suitcase Rule, I found the emphasis on "undersharing" and dissembling to be stifling—and a golden opportunity for rebellion.

The first memoir I read was Christina Crawford's *Mommie Dearest*, which I devoured my freshman year of high school. I was fascinated by the younger Crawford's conscious and public act of disloyalty to her mother and to the code of not airing dirty laundry outside the family. The book inspired my first public efforts at memoir in drama class. When it came time to deliver monologues, I mined funny and shocking family stories to great effect. The stunned laughter I got in response to my transgressive narratives convinced me I was onto something. I could tell truths that felt liberating to tell—and I could hold an audience at the same time. That was a compelling and seductive combination.

What I learned in these early performances was something that carried over into my later writing: Revelations that focus on one's own past, no matter how intimate, are always safer than ones that involve other people's stories. In 2006, I wrote a blog post about getting circumcised at age thirty-seven. I explained why I'd taken this step, sharing a few explicit anecdotes about how my foreskin often failed to retract fully during sex. I revealed nothing about anyone else. The post was picked up by *New York* magazine, first in print and then online, and eventually led to an appearance on *The Ricki Lake Show*. It also led to a lot of teasing and quite a few eye rolls. What it didn't lead to was anger. No one else could claim that his or her privacy had been violated.

The circumcision story proved to be one of the few pieces of mini-memoir I could write that didn't involve telling other people's stories alongside my own. My subsequent public violations of the Suitcase Rule would be more controversial, as I made the more difficult choice to write a series of pieces about ex-wives (I've been married four times) and girlfriends. On my own blog, and later at sites like *xoJane* and *Jezebel*, I offered a series of true stories about some of the more memorable incidents from past relationships.

I wrote about my second wife, who came out as a lesbian after our divorce but who had remained stubbornly closeted through our courtship and marriage. I wrote about the time that my third wife, after we had already made the decision to get a divorce, asked for my help removing a stuck tampon. I wrote about a student with whom I had been romantically involved and how she told me after our affair was over how badly our sexual relationship had damaged her sense of her own academic ability. And I wrote about a troubled ex-girlfriend whom I had tried to kill in an act of murder-suicide while we were both in the midst of a weeklong drug binge.

In each of these stories, I wrote about my own feelings of bewilderment or arousal or rage or guilt. I wrote about how confused I'd been by my second wife's sexuality and the mix of relief, shock, and sudden clarity I'd experienced when I learned that she'd come out. I explained how while struggling to remove my third wife's tampon, I'd felt empathy and arousal competing for primacy in my mind. I shared the chilling details of the moment I decided to kill myself and my ex-girlfriend so that we might find comfort together in the life to come. These were, I felt sure, my stories to tell. Even if, or perhaps especially if, they cast me in a less-than-flattering light.

I never contacted any of these women for permission to write about them. By the time each of these stories was published, I'd long since lost touch with their co-subjects. Though my third wife might have been willing to have a catch-up chat on the phone, I knew that the other women involved would not want to hear from me. At the same time, I chose not to contact them, not out of fear that they'd be adamantly opposed to me sharing these stories and anecdotes but because I didn't think I needed to do so. As long as I made an effort to disguise their identities, I had the right to share the truth with or without their consent. Or so I believed.

These stories had shaped me, too. Weren't they also mine to tell?

The reaction at sites like *Jezebel, xoJane,* and *Role Reboot* was almost uniformly negative. There were many impassioned debates on the ethics of memoir in the discussion sections that accompanied the articles. Most readers—at least those who bothered to comment—weren't buying the "if it happened to you, it's your story to tell" defense. At least, they weren't buying it in the case of the stories I'd written.

One point stuck with me: There's a distinction between relating "what happened to you" and sharing the story of "what you chose to do." The commenters set up a dichotomy, one that I hadn't considered, between "good" and "bad" memoir. "Good" memoir, like *Mommie Dearest,* described suffering through a victim's eyes. Bad—or at least morally questionable—memoir was either written from the perspective of a perpetrator, or it told the story of someone else's pain without that person's prior consent. A few participants in the discussions pointed out laws in many states that bar murderers from profiting from memoirs about their crimes. That same principle, they suggested, ought to apply to memoirs written by anyone who could be considered abusive. A man who wrote about trying to kill his ex-girlfriend, or who merely related an embarrassing gynecological anecdote about an ex-wife without her consent, might reasonably be declared an abusive memoirist.

Collectively the negative reaction to these slices of memoir was overwhelming. It shook me badly. Eventually the hostile reaction (justified or not) was strong enough to lead me to choose to take an extended break from writing online or anywhere else.

I've had ample opportunity to reconsider what it means to write about a past that includes other people's stories as well as one's own. I've been tempted to agree with those who argue that memoir rightly belongs to the marginalized and to the previously silenced. I now think that when it's possible to do so, the kind, if not essential, thing is for a writer to gain permission—or at least give a fair warning—to the person whose story will be told.

In the end, there is no perfect moral calculus for balancing one person's right to tell his or her story with others' right to privacy. The right to privacy does not automatically trump the right to share. Staying silent for the sake of preserving harmony or protecting another's feelings may well be a valid choice for a would-be memoirist. The Suitcase Rule, writ large, keeps the peace. Yet without stories that are both true and transgressive, we miss out on rich insights into the human experience. And without memoir that dares to offend—or that risks opening old wounds—we lose the precious opportunity to recognize our most private selves in the stories others tell.

Hugo Schwyzer was a history and gender-studies professor at Pasadena City College from 1993–2013. A former weekly columnist for *Jezebel*, *The Atlantic*, and *Daily Life* (Australia), Hugo's work has also appeared in *xoJane*, *The Times of Israel*, *The Guardian*, the *Los Angeles Times*, and many other outlets. Hugo co-authored *Beauty, Disrupted: A Memoir* (It Books/HarperCollins, 2011) with famed supermodel Carré Otis. In the aftermath of a very public 2013 breakdown, Hugo went on a semipermanent hiatus from writing and lecturing. The father of two children, he lives in Los Angeles.

HONORING DEATH
Naseem Rakha

It was mid-January 2013, two weeks before I was to head out for a one-month artist-in-residence stay at the Grand Canyon, when I read about a young woman who had gone missing while rafting the Colorado River through the mile-deep chasm. Her name was Kaitlin, and halfway through her twenty-nine-day river trip, her group woke to find her gone.

I know the Colorado River. I know how cold it is. How swift. How unforgiving it can be to the slightest bit of arrogance or carelessness or banality. And I assumed, when I read about the missing girl, that she would not be found alive. The river and its canyon are simply not that kind. But I also know how full and fulfilling a river trip through the canyon can be. How it changes lives and perspectives, making people bigger and stronger while simultaneously dwarfing them with the immensity of time and space and the gathering eclipses they will never see.

To raft the Colorado through its nearly two-billion-year-old rocks, or hike the narrow paths that lead to and beside the river, is to be a part of the world in the most sublime sense. Like sand is part of the world, and water and tree and root. There is healing in the canyon. And challenge. And art and glory and a quiet that fills your mind and then spreads through every cell to every limb. I have felt it, have seen it, and know it to be true.

Kaitlin was a student at the University of Montana studying Native American culture and anthropology. She was a wilderness backpacker, a master fiddler, and an accomplished dancer. How appropriate, then, that she should wind her way down to the bottom of the world's greatest canyon to be among the continent's oldest rocks and deepest history. A place where water dances and wrens sing and thunder echoes and color is born.

And so I wrote about the young woman I had never met. I wanted to say that though her disappearance is likely to end tragically, perhaps there is some comfort knowing that in all likelihood Kaitlin—who had chosen to spend her twenty-first birthday at the bottom of a cold canyon—was living a very big and full life right until the moment she was gone. I compared it to my own near-death experience inside the belly of the canyon. I was swept away by the water, battered down to the river bottom, flipped and turned and unable to grab a breath of air. I knew I was dying. And I knew it was sad. But then there was the revelation: If this was my time, then where better than the place I feel most alive?

I posted the essay on my blog and then two weeks later got in my car and drove to the Grand Canyon. During that three-day road trip, the National Park Service had changed its mission to find Kaitlin from "search and rescue" to simply "search." They were combing the waters for a body now, informing rafters to be on the lookout, particularly within eddies and other places that gather the flotsam that drifts down the river. Shortly after that, I began to hear from people I had never met: friends of Kaitlin's, distant relatives, teachers. Each one e-mailed to thank me for my post. It meant a lot, they said. It helped when little else did. Then, on the night before my first solo hike to canyon bottom, I heard from Kaitlin's "first love." He told me stories about the young woman. How magical she was. How she brought life and love and spirit into a room. No one could imagine her being gone. It did not seem right, and I felt myself being drawn into the young woman's story. I was living in one of the first homes built along the canyon. Each window looked out on the seventeen-mile-wide aroyo, and somewhere down there, beneath the water or waiting in some eddy, was Kaitlin.

I asked the young man if he would like me to make a memorial for his friend while I was at the river, and he said yes. So, when I reached the water, I gathered stones, drew a picture, and wrote a note to the missing woman. Feeling sad. Feeling alive. Feeling alone in the canyon's vastness. After I climbed back out to the rim world, I posted pictures of the memorial on my website, hoping it would reach the right people.

Four weeks later, I was back home. It was mid-March, and I received a phone call from Kaitlin's uncle. Kaitlin's body had been found, and he asked if I would be willing to speak to her parents. I was scared. Why would they want to speak with me? What could I possibly say to a grief that had to be so large? I reluctantly said yes. The next day, I received an e-mail from Kaitlin's father. He had attached several items and asked if I would call. I immediately closed my computer and went for a walk. The next morning I avoided my computer entirely. I still had no idea what I would say to this family. Then, in the afternoon, I finally got up the nerve and opened my computer.

The first attachment was the brochure from Kaitlin's memorial. On it was a photo of the beautiful young woman playing her violin. The next was a letter her mother read at the memorial. By now I was crying. The last attachment was Billy Collins's poem "Questions About Angels," in which Collins describes one single angel dancing on the head of a pin. The poem described the Kaitlin I had come to know. Beautiful. Free. Happy. Full of life. The poem was also read at her memorial, and just as I was reading it, my son put on the stereo and on came the Wailin' Jennys' song "Calling All Angels." I closed my computer and called Kaitlin's mother and father.

The awkwardness lasted maybe a minute. Then I told them about reading the poem and the music that came on, and they told me the song was one of Kaitlin's favorites. "A lot of things like that have been happening," her mother said. And then they told me about their daughter. She was the youngest, an unexpected gift who brought joy to every room she entered. They talked about what she loved to do, how she made people laugh and feel whole and bigger and better about themselves. I imagined her as one of those young women I see more and more of these days. Unencumbered by *should*s and *should not*s and unburdened by stereotype. Strong, and beautiful, she delighted people who understand life is short and precious and needs to be grabbed with both hands, cuddled, and loved.

We talked for an hour, with them telling me how much my two posts, the original one and then the one about the stone memorial, meant to them. Thousands of people had viewed the blog about Kaitlin. For Kaitlin's parents it was a raft—a place they could go and read a story about their daughter that they wanted others to read and understand as well—a safe and guarded place—and I felt grateful that I was able to create that.

Before we hung up, they asked if I would consider writing one more post about Kaitlin. This one, telling people Kaitlin had been found. I said yes, and within a day, the family had sent me her river journal, pictures of her growing up, poems she had written, drawings. I was the repository of memories. And I knew it was one of the most important writing assignments I had ever been given, and one of the most emotionally powerful. Throughout the day, Kaitlin was at my side. I could feel her in the music her parents sent me, see her in the pictures, and I felt such deep, deep sorrow as the words fell out and the story was told.

A month later, *The Oregonian* wanted an essay about how writing can affect others. Then *Outside* magazine picked up the story of Kaitlin's odyssey of going out in search of the wild, of reaching into and out of her life, of her beauty and earnestness, and of the price she paid to live fully.

In December of this year, I had the honor to actually meet Kaitlin's parents. I was in Denver, and they invited me to their home. Kaitlin's brother, sister, and niece were there as well, as were some friends. One of them played Kaitlin's fiddle for me. It was strange, sad, and beautiful. Pulling, like water will.

People often ask where stories come from. My answer: Just open your eyes, your heart, and your mind. People often ask what stories can do. My answer: Just open your eyes, your heart, and your mind. Then put your pen to paper and breathe ...

Naseem Rakha lives in Silverton, Oregon, with her son, husband, and animals. She is the author of the international bestseller *The Crying Tree*. When not writing, Naseem is hiking, gardening, reading, and figuring out ways to get herself back to the Colorado Plateau.

Appendix

SELECT BOOKS ON WRITING MEMOIRS

Family Trouble: Memoirists on the Hazards and Rewards of Revealing Family
by Joy Castro

In *Family Trouble,* Joy Castro helps navigate the tricky terrain of the family memoir. In essays by twenty-five memoirists, Faith Adiele, Alison Bechdel, Jill Christman, Rigoberto González, Dinty W. Moore, and others share their varied experiences with memoir writing while emphasizing the importance of telling these stories. Castro provides a comprehensive look at the quandaries inherent in telling family secrets, while offering writers practical strategies for balancing the truth of their own stories with family loyalties and boundaries.

Fearless Confessions: A Writer's Guide to Memoir
by Sue William Silverman

Sue William Silverman's *Fearless Confessions* is an essential resource for beginning and accomplished writers alike. *Fearless Confessions* draws on diverse experiences, clear instruction, and writing exercises to engage writers throughout the writing process. Spanning topics ranging from the craft elements to the marketing and publication of a memoir, Silverman provides an invaluable blueprint for confronting the challenges of putting our powerful experiences on the page.

Your Life as Story: Discovering the "New Autobiography" and Writing Memoir as Literature
by Tristine Rainer

In *Your Life as Story*, Tristine Rainer dispels the myth that worthwhile memoirs belong solely to the realm of celebrity. Instead Rainer emphasizes the vital importance of the narratives that shape our lives and the meaning we derive from our personal stories. Complete with practical advice and directed exercises, *Your Life as Story* gives writers the tools to develop a fundamental structure from lived experiences.

The Situation and the Story: The Art of Personal Narrative
by Vivian Gornick

The Situation and the Story provides writers with an in-depth look at what makes a personal narrative work. Drawing on excerpts by a wide variety of essay and memoir writers, Gornick teaches writers how to read as well as write memoir. Her entertaining and thorough deconstruction of the writing process makes *The Situation and the Story* a great resource for writers who wish to understand the essence of the personal narratives in our pivotal experiences.

The Passionate, Accurate Story: Making Your Heart's Truth into Literature
by Carol Bly

As the title implies, *The Passionate, Accurate Story* encourages writers to move beyond the technical aspects of craft into the murkier issues that make for emotionally, intellectually, and morally rich writing. Though primarily aimed at short-story writers, Bly's attention to the conscious and unconscious realities of our lives, and subsequently our stories, is a valuable resource for writers who want to translate that complex passion onto the page.

Reality Hunger: A Manifesto
by David Shields

David Shields's *Reality Hunger* tackles one of the most prevalent artistic issues of our time: Why are we as a culture so obsessed with realism? By examining the multiple facets of this question, Shields provides a vital discussion on the impact of reality's central role in writing and publishing today as well as the possibilities for the future of this art form. By challenging some long-held notions about literature, Shields provides writers with a look at its evolution, with particular relevance to memoir as a genre drawn from lived experience.

Tell It Slant: Writing and Shaping Creative Nonfiction
by Brenda Miller and Suzanne Paola

Tell It Slant offers a comprehensive look at writing and honing the craft of creative nonfiction. With over thirty essays by Margaret Atwood, David Sedaris, E.B. White, and others, Miller and Paola provide an impressive anthology as well as writing exercises to guide writers through the process of developing and refining their work. Miller and Paola's thorough yet practical examination of creative nonfiction gives writers the strategies necessary to shape their work as well as experiment with the various forms that creative nonfiction has to offer.

Naked, Drunk, and Writing: Shed Your Inhibitions and Craft a Compelling Memoir or Personal Essay
by Adair Lara

In *Naked, Drunk, and Writing*, Adair Lara draws on her experience as a writer, editor, and teacher to help aspiring writers get their story written. Lara provides practical advice that covers all the essentials of beginning your memoir, such as the importance of narrative conflict, while also addressing issues like writing routines, discipline, and how to submit your work and get published. *Naked, Drunk, and Writing's* entertaining and engaging tone and practical guidance are sure to inspire you throughout the writing process.

The Heroine's Journey: Woman's Quest for Wholeness
by Maureen Murdock

The Heroine's Journey is an insightful look at the cultural narratives that affect women's lives. Particularly valuable to writers covering women's issues, Murdock draws on social myths and symbols, in addition to her own life as a mother, therapist, and writer, to guide both readers and writers alike through a process of healing and empowerment. Murdock's compassionate and multilevel examination of culture and feminine values serves as a wonderful example of how to construct the seemingly scattered pieces of one's life into a powerful and meaningful story.

Handling the Truth: On the Writing of Memoir
by Beth Kephart

Drawing from the work and experience of many authors and students, *Handling the Truth* is a genuine and endearing look at the meaning and value of writing memoir. Kephart presents aspiring writers with the encouragement needed to embrace their stories, while honestly addressing the pitfalls and rewards of the writing life. Combining both discussions on the importance of memoir with thought-provoking instruction, *Handling the Truth* is an important resource for writers looking to add depth and detail to their work.

Bird by Bird: Some Instructions on Writing and Life
by Anne Lamott

In *Bird by Bird*, Anne Lamott presents an inspiring, vivid, and comical look at the ups and downs of the writing life, and fast-paced instruction that encourages writers to bring forth their story. With chapters like "How Do You Know When You're Done?" and "Writer's Block," Lamott offers insight into writers' struggles with self-doubt, perfectionism, and completing the first draft, while emphasizing that the value in writing far exceeds just getting published.

Inventing the Truth: The Art and Craft of Memoir
by William Zinsser

In *Inventing the Truth*, William Zinsser and several contributing memoirists offer their advice on the task of writing about one's life. Focusing on truth's relationship to the story, Zinsser and others offer advice about whose truth belongs in memoir and the process of having that truth analyzed. *Inventing the Truth* also offers advice on the intersections of technique, experience, and fact that is valuable for writers trying to navigate the sometimes cloudy waters of memoir writing.

I Could Tell You Stories: Sojourns in the Land of Memory
by Patricia Hampl

Patricia Hampl presents an insightful look into memoir and storytelling through a set of essays that investigate the works of notable memoirists like Czeslaw Milosz, Edith Stein, Sylvia Plath, Walt Whitman, and others. *I Could Tell You Stories* is a rich guide for the exploration of memory, ethics, and emotional truth that illustrates how to draw a narrative arc from seemingly unimportant, everyday occurrences. It reminds us of the importance of truth and meaning in the written life.

The Made-Up Self: Impersonation in the Personal Essay
by Carl H. KIaus

In *The Made-Up Self*, Carl H. Klaus provides an in-depth study of the personal essay that addresses issues such as the peculiar role of the "I" and its impact on different facets of craft, technique, and reception. Drawing on the works of such authors as Michel de Montaigne, Charles Lamb, E.B. White, and Virginia Woolf, Klaus illustrates how culture, persona, personal experience, and crafting all play a role in the personal essay's complex development.

Writing as a Way of Healing: How Telling Our Stories Transforms Our Lives
by Louise DeSalvo

In *Writing as a Way of Healing*, Louise DeSalvo examines the relationship between trauma, healing, and writing. DeSalvo emphasizes the accessibility and role of writing as a healing tool for both readers and writers, and how it helps people decode and transcend traumas by linking events, feelings, and the self together in a coherent way. From the spark of a story in a journal to a writer's attempt at publication, *Writing as a Way of Healing* is filled with the techniques and guidance that help readers and writers better understand themselves and others.

Crafting the Personal Essay: A Guide for Writing and Publishing Creative Nonfiction
by Dinty W. Moore

Dinty W. Moore's *Crafting the Personal Essay* is a hands-on guide to writing creative nonfiction and is chock-full of exercises, examples, and tips on writing and publishing the personal essay. Spanning memoir, travel, humor, nature essays, and more, Moore's guide gives writers the tools to find the vital insights and themes in their experience, construct their writing, and revise for publication. *Crafting the Personal Essay* is a practical guide for writers looking to find the universal meaning in their individual stories.

Thinking About Memoir
by Abigail Thomas

In *Thinking About Memoir*, Abigail Thomas, in conjunction with AARP and Sterling Publishing, presents a thoughtful look at writing as a means to understand the events of our lives and shed some light on how we grew into ourselves. Thomas draws on her personal and professional experience to give writers honest and poignant advice on locating the details and honing the creative habits and structural sensibilities that are sure to inspire writers to see new possibilities in their own writing.

To Show and to Tell: The Craft of Literary Nonfiction
by Phillip Lopate

To Show and to Tell is an indispensable guide to memoir and personal essay that challenges writers to go beyond the simple and sage. Starting with the nuts and bolts of writing literary nonfiction, Lopate considers these forms in cultural and psychological contexts. Providing humorous and frank advice on the technical (craft, skill, technique) and psychological challenges ("self-hatred" and "guilt") of writing, Lopate's guide offers the tools needed to confront the more vexing aspects of writing literary nonfiction.

Writing the Memoir: From Truth to Art
by Judith Barrington

Writing the Memoir is an in-depth, explanatory look at the unique challenges that memoir writers face, from following an idea through to its publication to technical problems like voice, scene, character development, and beyond. Barrington draws from the writings of Alice Walker, Kathleen Norris, Annie Dillard, Frank Conroy, and Virginia Woolf, as well as her personal experience with memoir, to teach writers to balance the emotional honesty of their lived experience with artistic skill to build powerful narratives. The book also includes writing exercises and advice on the dilemmas of writing about others.

The Power of Memoir: How to Write Your Healing Story
by Linda Joy Myers

The Power of Memoir provides writers with a step-by-step guide to writing memoir as a healing process. Myers's gentle voice and thorough approach for accessing painful as well as empowering memories provides writers with the tools and exercises to develop their experiences into a meaningful, structured story. *The Power of Memoir* also includes sections on whether or not to publish a memoir and a variety of examples from Myers's students that illustrate both the technical, healing, and creative aspects of memoir writing.

MEMOIRS BY AUTHORS MENTIONED IN THIS BOOK (AND SELECTED RECOMMENDATIONS)

Trash by Dorothy Allison

Two or Three Things I Know for Sure by Dorothy Allison

Candyfreak: A Journey Through the Chocolate Underbelly of America by Steve Almond

Rock and Roll Will Save Your Life by Steve Almond

I Know Why the Caged Bird Sings by Maya Angelou

Hungry for the World: A Memoir by Kim Barnes

In the Wilderness: Coming of Age in Unknown Country by Kim Barnes

Lifesaving: A Memoir by Judith Barrington

Are You My Mother?: A Comic Drama by Alison Bechdel

Fun Home: A Family Tragicomic by Alison Bechdel

The Rules of Inheritance: A Memoir by Claire Bidwell Smith

Telling Secrets: A Memoir by Frederick Buechner

A Wolf at the Table by Augusten Burroughs

Dry: A Memoir by Augusten Burroughs

Magical Thinking: True Stories by Augusten Burroughs

Possible Side Effects by Augusten Burroughs

Running with Scissors: A Memoir by Augusten Burroughs

Let's Take the Long Way Home: A Memoir of Friendship by Gail Caldwell

Opium: The Diary of His Cure by Jean Cocteau

Poser: My Life in Twenty-Three Yoga Poses by Claire Dederer

After Henry by Joan Didion

Blue Nights by Joan Didion

Miami by Joan Didion

Political Fictions by Joan Didion

Salvador by Joan Didion

Slouching Towards Bethlehem by Joan Didion

The White Album: Essays by Joan Didion

The Year of Magical Thinking by Joan Didion

We Tell Ourselves Stories in Order to Live: Collected Nonfiction by
    Joan Didion

Where I Was From by Joan Didion

Loving Lampposts (documentary) by Todd Drezner

Not By Accident: Reconstructing a Careless Life by Samantha Dunn

The Possibility of Everything: A Memoir by Hope Edelman

*A Heartbreaking Work of Staggering Genius: A Memoir Based on a
    True Story* by Dave Eggers

*A Match to the Heart: One Woman's Story of Being Struck by Light-
    ning* by Gretel Ehrlich

The Solace of Open Spaces by Gretel Ehrlich

Screw Everyone: Sleeping My Way to Monogamy by Ophira Eisenberg

Whip Smart: The True Story of a Secret Life by Melissa Febos

Tiger, Tiger: A Memoir by Margaux Fragoso

Autobiography of a Face by Lucy Grealy

Hurry Down Sunshine: A Memoir by Michael Greenberg

Sickened: The True Story of a Lost Childhood by Julie Gregory

*Live Through This: A Mother's Memoir of Runaway Daughters and
    Reclaimed Love* by Debra Gwartney

The Florist's Daughter by Patricia Hampl

Crazy Brave: A Memoir by Joy Harjo

The Kiss: A Memoir by Kathryn Harrison

The Mother Knot: A Memoir by Kathryn Harrison

While They Slept: An Inquiry into the Murder of a Family by Kath-
    ryn Harrison

The Woman Warrior: Memoirs of a Girlhood Among Ghosts by
    Maxine Hong Kingston

Madness: A Bipolar Life by Marya Hornbacher

Wasted: A Memoir of Anorexia and Bulimia by Marya Hornbacher

Love Him Madly: An Intimate Memoir of Jim Morrison by Judy
    Huddleston

The Stuff of Life: A Daughter's Memoir by Karen Karbo

Cherry: A Memoir by Mary Karr
Lit: A Memoir by Mary Karr
The Liars' Club: A Memoir by Mary Karr
Girl, Interrupted by Susanna Kaysen
The Camera My Mother Gave Me by Susanna Kaysen
Drinking: A Love Story by Caroline Knapp
Bird by Bird: Some Instructions on Writing and Life by Anne Lamott
Some Girls: My Life in a Harem by Jillian Lauren
This Is How You Say Goodbye: A Daughter's Memoir by Victoria
    Loustalot
Something Wrong with Her: A Real-Time Memoir by Cris Mazza
Circles Around the Sun: In Search of a Lost Brother by Molly
    McCloskey
The Tender Bar: A Memoir by J.R. Moehringer
*Don't Call Me Mother: A Daughter's Journey from Abandonment to
    Forgiveness* by Linda Joy Myers
Speak, Memory by Vladimir Nabokov
Reading Lolita in Tehran by Azar Nafisi
Silences by Tillie Olsen
Her: A Memoir by Christa Parravani
Truth & Beauty by Ann Patchett
Loud in the House of Myself: Memoir of a Strange Girl by Stacy
    Pershall
Private Lies: Infidelity and the Betrayal of Intimacy by Frank Pittman
Wedlocked: A Memoir by Jay Ponteri
The Survival of the Coolest by William Pryor
Love Junkie: A Memoir by Rachel Resnick
Schuyler's Monster: A Father's Journey with His Wordless Daughter
    by Robert C. Rummel-Hudson
A Common Pornography: A Memoir by Kevin Sampsell
Jesus Land by Julia Scheeres
Me Talk Pretty One Day by David Sedaris

Making Peace with Autism: One Family's Story of Struggle, Discovery, and Unexpected Gifts by Susan Senator
Devotion: A Memoir by Dani Shapiro
Slow Motion: A Memoir of a Life Rescued by Tragedy by Dani Shapiro
Five Men Who Broke My Heart by Susan Shapiro
Lighting Up: How I Stopped Smoking, Drinking, and Everything Else I Loved in Life Except Sex by Susan Shapiro
Love and Exile: An Autobiographical Trilogy by Isaac Bashevis Singer
Lying: A Metaphorical Memoir by Lauren Slater
Welcome to My Country: A Therapist's Memoir of Madness by Lauren Slater
House Rules: A Memoir by Rachel Sontag
Tiny Beautiful Things: Advice on Love and Life from Dear Sugar by Cheryl Strayed
Wild: From Lost to Found on the Pacific Crest Trail by Cheryl Strayed
Darkness Visible: A Memoir of Madness by William Styron
Hotels, Hospitals, and Jails: A Memoir by Anthony Swofford
Jarhead: A Marine's Chronicle of the Gulf War and Other Battles by Anthony Swofford
A Three Dog Life by Abigail Thomas
Down These Mean Streets by Piri Thomas
Because I Remember Terror, Father, I Remember You by Sue William Silverman
Love Sick: One Woman's Journey Through Sexual Addiction by Sue William Silverman
This Boy's Life: A Memoir by Tobias Wolff
A House with No Roof: After My Father's Assassination, A Memoir by Rebecca Wilson
More, Now, Again: A Memoir of Addiction by Elizabeth Wurtzel
Prozac Nation by Elizabeth Wurtzel
Chronology of Water: A Memoir by Lidia Yuknavitch
Smashed: Story of a Drunken Girlhood by Koren Zailckas

MEMOIRS BY THE ESSAY AUTHORS WHO APPEAR IN THIS BOOK

Ariel Gore
The End of Eve: A Memoir
Atlas of the Human Heart: A Memoir

Ona Gritz
On the Whole: A Story of Mothering and Disability

Traci Foust
Nowhere Near Normal: A Memoir of OCD

Ben Tanzer
Lost in Space: A Father's Journey There and Back Again

Carolyn Roy-Bornstein
Crash: A Mother, A Son, and the Journey from Grief to Gratitude

Cris Mazza
Something Wrong with Her: A Real-Time Memoir

Rachel Ament
The Jewish Daughter Diaries: True Stories of Being Loved Too Much By Our Moms (editor)

Sheila Hageman
Stripping Down: A Memoir

Nicole Hardy
Confessions of a Latter-Day Virgin: A Memoir

Janet Hardy
Girlfag: A Life Told in Sex and Musicals

Erica Rivera
Insatiable: A Young Mother's Struggle with Anorexia

Vincent Truman
Departnered: A Virtual Memoir of Marriage, Divorce, and Pixels

Ellen Currey-Wilson
The Big Turnoff: Confessions of a TV-Addicted Mom Trying to Raise a TV-Free Kid

Hugo Schwyzer
Beauty, Disrupted: A Memoir (with Carré Otis)

INDEX